0020955 R3 £3.95

PRISON CRISIS

By the same author
THE POLICE REVOLUTION
THE PROTEST VIRUS
THE BLACK MAN IN SEARCH OF POWER (joint author)
ATTITUDES OF YOUNG IMMIGRANTS (with Marplan)
PUBLISH AND BE DAMNED?

Prison Crisis

by
PETER EVANS
Foreword by SIR ROBERT MARK

London
GEORGE ALLEN & UNWIN
Boston   Sydney

First published in 1980

This book is copyright under the Berne Convention. All rights are reserved. Apart from any fair dealing for the purpose of private study, research, criticism or review, as permitted under the Copyright Act, 1956, no part of this publication may be reproduced, stored in a retrieval system, or transmitted, in any form or by any means, electronic, electrical, chemical, mechanical, optical, photocopying, recording or otherwise, without the prior permission of the copyright owner. Enquiries should be sent to the publishers at the undermentioned address:

GEORGE ALLEN & UNWIN LTD
40 Museum Street, London WC1A 1LU

© Peter Evans

British Library Cataloguing in Publication Data

Evans, Peter
   Prison crisis.
   1. Prisons – Great Britain
   I. Title
   365'.941   HV9647   80–40543

ISBN 0–04–365003–1
ISBN 0–04–365004–X

Typeset in 11 on 12 point Baskerville by Trade Linotype Ltd, Birmingham
and printed in Great Britain
by Lowe & Brydone Limited, Thetford, Norfolk

To my mother, 80 this year

Foreword
by Sir Robert Mark, G.B.E., Q.P.M.

This is a particularly welcome and long overdue book. It is written by a layman for laymen about a complex and controversial subject, the prison system about which many politicians, academics and social workers pretend knowledge but of which few have actual experience. Indeed, there can be few, if any, subjects on which so much influential comment is made by people unqualified to shape public opinion, and only too often this is done without any reference to those best able to inform them, the Prison Service itself.

The book raises all sorts of issues, any one of which could and should be of great interest to a caring public. What should be the purpose or purposes of a prison system in the late twentieth century? Is it possible to reconcile the conflicting aims of discipline, in the sense in which the Prison Service uses that word, and treatment, or rehabilitation? What sort of prison service is necessary to meet the diverse requirements which, in theory at least, are expected of it? How accountable should that service be and to whom? Should information about prison conditions be more widely available? Do the politicians and civil servants of the Home Office administer so controversial and difficult a system properly? Does the evidence of recent years afford any encouragement? Is financial stringency likely to deny any real prospect of doing more than coping with the conflicting needs of a widely varying prison population on a day-to-day basis?

My reaction to the book is that of a layman who cannot pretend deep knowledge of our penal system and of prisons in particular, though the two months I spent as assessor to Lord Mountbatten's Inquiry into Prison Security in 1966 enabled me to visit some seventeen prisons of various kinds, and my police service had given me the opportunity to visit others, notably Strangeways and Walton. Even so, I suspect that I have a little more knowledge of the actuality of the prison system and the vicissitudes of the Prison

x   *Prison Crisis*

Service than some of those who feel competent to advise the Home Secretary and educate the public about both. It is not all that hazardous to offer advice which is never tested by evidence submitted to judicial inquiry or public opinion. In a nutshell, that is the essential difference between a Special Branch officer and an ordinary detective in peacetime. The work of the latter is continually subject to test, that of the former, scarcely, if ever. For that and other reasons I agree with the author that information about the prison system should be much more widely available to the public – and, I stress, the public, not just politicians. Worthwhile reforms unattractive to those in power or jealously protecting a vested interest are unlikely without the weight of public opinion. The introduction of majority verdicts in 1967 against weighty opposition from the lawyers both in and out of Parliament is surely a classic demonstration of that.

More and better information about prisons would benefit not only the occupants but the Prison Service itself. The public simply does not understand the difficulties faced by both. Mr Evans describes eloquently the evils – and that is not too strong a word – of overcrowding. It is a significant comment on our politicians that many prisoners today are housed in conditions which late-Victorian criminals would find thoroughly familiar.

It is, of course, difficult indeed to apply modern standards to a prison population which tends to increase rather than diminish. There are two obvious courses to follow: the first, to make less use of the custodial sentence; the second, to build more prisons better adapted for diversified purposes. In fact, we have done fairly well in avoiding use of the custodial sentence. If we applied today the sentencing standards of eighty years ago the prison population would soon be doubled, with even more hardship for both prisoners and the prison service. The urgent need to keep to the lowest possible level the number of those in custody has not always, however, reflected every aspect of the public interest. The author comments, by implication critically, on the acquittal, or the disposal without a custodial sentence, of 51 per cent of those denied liberty whilst awaiting trial. There is another side to that question, which government itself is not anxious to pursue and, indeed, seems almost willing to conceal, namely the extent and gravity of crimes committed by those on bail, often against police objection. It is probably

Foreword xi

right that there should be a prescriptive right to bail in the great majority of cases. It is surely no less right that there should be a prescriptive denial of bail in some cases, to be waived only by a judge. Most cases of violence, especially robbery, the use of firearms or other weapons in the pursuance of crime, should clearly fall within the latter category. As for those acquitted after remand in custody, ought not redress to be assessed as a routine measure by a court examination of the evidence on which denial of liberty was ordered?

Mr Evans comments on the problems arising from the dispersal of prisoners of high security risk throughout closed prisons generally. I must confess an interest. Lord Mountbatten saw this recommendation as opening the door to a more liberal and relaxed system for the great majority of prisoners. He went to some pains to express his view that top-security prisoners would be less of a problem if housed in humane conditions and that special consideration could more easily be given to their requirements and those of the staff responsible for them. To many with knowledge of the Prison Service this made good sense. The political hubbub following Blake's escape having subsided, the idea never got off the ground. It would be interesting to know how many prison officers were asked to comment. The result is the worst of all possible worlds, with our most hardened criminals enjoying extensive opportunity to contaminate the rest of the prison population not in open establishments, helped by the unnecessarily restrictive conditions imposed by dispersal.

I do not share the view discussed in the book and urged by Lord Mountbatten that an easily identifiable and prestigious head of the Prison Service would make any real difference to its status or contentment. Lord Mountbatten contemplated for the Prison Service a kind of Chief Inspector of Constabulary, enjoying considerable status, with access to the minister and the media, and thus able to raise the morale of the service by ensuring consideration of their views. I do not think the problem can be resolved in that way. It is one of system, not individuals. The Prison Service does not have the triple accountability of the police – to the courts, to local police authorities and to the Home Secretary. It does not enjoy the freedom of the police from political or bureaucratic influence in operational matters. The Chief Inspector of Constabulary, though always a distinguished former policeman respected by the service, has minimal influence on those issues in which chief police officers feel that the well-being of the police service is involved. The police service is constitutionally able to speak for itself and to gain a public hearing. The Prison Service, by contrast, is unquestionably the responsibility of the Home Secretary alone. He clearly cannot divest himself of any part of it. What he could do with advantage, I suspect, is to allow and encourage wider and more frequent discussion of the problems of the Prison Service with representatives chosen by prison officers themselves. I should have thought, for example, that representatives of security prisons, open prisons and borstals should have been elected by their colleagues to the Standing Advisory Council on the Penal System from the outset. The unquestioned accountability of the Prison Service to the Home Secretary alone should not deprive it of the right – indeed, the duty on occasion – to express publicly opinions or advice he might find politically or otherwise unwelcome. It is the lack of this facility and tradition, rather than of a charismatic leader, which I suspect gives rise to frustration and resentment.

I am not one of those who think that harsher treatment and longer sentences are likely to reduce the prison population. They would certainly make the lot of the Prison Service even harder and would probably affect adversely the standard of entrant. Those who urge such policies usually do so as an emotional rather than a logical reaction to public anger and frustration arising from the increase in crime, particularly violent crime, and the occasional failure of the justice system in particular cases.

It is too easy to blame dissatisfaction with our prisons on convenient scapegoats. However critically the achievements of the Home Office and its civil servants are viewed, I do not think a reasonable observer could doubt the honesty or humanity of their intentions in the post-war years. As long ago as 1910, when he was Home Secretary, Winston Churchill said in the House of Commons:

> The mood and temper of the public with regard to the treatment of crime and criminals is one of the unfailing tests of the civilization of any country. A calm, dispassionate recognition

of the rights of the accused – and even of the convicted – criminal against the State; a constant heart-searching by all charged with the duty of punishment; a desire and eagerness to rehabilitate in the world of industry those who have paid their due in the hard coinage of punishment; tireless efforts towards the discovery of curative and regenerative processes; unfailing faith that there is a treasure, if you can only find it, in the heart of every man; these are the symbols which, in the treatment of crime and criminal, mark and measure the stored-up strength of a nation and are a sign and proof of the living virtue in it.

If, seventy years later, we are still far short of that ideal, it is certainly not for want of trying. The practical difficulties are immense, not least of them expenditure on a scale that no government these days can meet. It is right, however, to attempt a perspective. With all the present difficulties and dissatisfactions, there has been much progress, particularly in the avoidance of the custodial sentence, the creation of open prisons, the extension of parole. Many of these changes attract criticism, sometimes through failure of judgement in a particular case rather than of policy. If it is undoubtedly true that conditions of prisoners are such as no civilised society ought to tolerate, it is also true that the Prison Service continues to lack the rewards and inducements necessary to attract the personnel able to attempt to fulfil its highest ideals. Law and order is an expensive business. It has always been well to the fore on the hustings, in the Commons and on television. It has always been well to the rear when government expenditure is apportioned. Only when it touches the public are the purse strings likely to loosen. Thus the police have had to be given two 40 per cent pay rises in sixteen years, having lost millions of pounds in the intervening years through the premature loss of trained manpower. Lord Edmund-Davies, chairman of the independent inquiry committee which recommended pay rises for the police in 1978, public opinion, and the good sense of Margaret Thatcher have at long last afforded real hope for the future. If the problems, anxieties and aspirations of the Prison Service are given a similar airing, perhaps it too could begin a new era in which it might for the first time enjoy the conditions necessary to attract and retain the quality of manpower necessary to realise its ideals.

The real value of Mr Evans's book is that it enables the ordinary, uninformed but interested citizen to begin to understand that prison is not just the end process of television drama. It is just as relevant to the standards of our society as Churchill said it was all those years ago.

Table of Contents

Foreword by Sir Robert Mark		*page*	ix
Author's Preface			xvii
1	The Crisis Dawns		1
2	Overcrowding		12
3	The Prisoners		21
	Terrorism – Life Sentences and Parole – Sentencing – Dispersal		
4	Abnormal Offenders		33
5	Young People in Custody		45
6	Women in Prison		57
7	Prisoners' Rights		66
	Control – Drugs – Confinement – Discipline		
8	Riots		83
9	Prison Officers protest		94
10	The Role of Whitehall		110
11	The May Inquiry		123
	Tackling the Home Office – Dealing with the Prisons		
12	Rescuing the Prisons		144
	Sentencing – Prison Administration – Staff – Boards of Visitors – Pay for Prisoners – Family Contacts – Secrecy – A New Rule		
Appendix: List of Members of the May Committee			160
References			162

Author's Preface

This book was conceived during the period when *The Times* was off the streets as a result of its industrial dispute, and its gestation period was approximately the same as that of the May Committee's Report, published in October 1979, which it takes into account. But the thought that has gone into this book began many years ago after my first visits to prisons, for during the last nine years when I have been Home Affairs Correspondent of *The Times* I have been given a greater consciousness of what is right and wrong with the system, a consciousness that has come mainly from what other people have had to say over a wide range of opinion as well as from my own observation.

Coincidentally, this has also been the period during which the crisis facing the Prison Service has become more acute, but, because the book necessarily dwells on the faults that have led to the crisis, I do not mean to imply that there is nothing right with the system. There are many dedicated people working, some in groups and others in isolation, whom I must also thank for help in broadening my mind to the possibilities which lie ahead if the faults are put right. That will take much money and much time – more than the lifetime of any single Government. It must therefore require vision and an act of faith. But if these are not forthcoming I genuinely fear for the consequences. There is much talent within and without the Prison Service and the Home Office which could be harnessed, given the will and the right leadership. And I say this despite my criticism of what has happened to damage the prison system to the detriment of prisoners and staff.

I wish to thank all those who have helped my understanding, whether they are in universities, the Home Office, prisons or organisations like the National Association for the Care and Resettlement of Offenders and the Howard League for Penal Reform; the information which they have provided over the years is distilled here. Many people in the Prison Service and others working alongside them have given me new insight into how prisons work and they deserve my special thanks.

It was a prison officer who, speaking of prisoners, said that people who hate themselves sometimes need most compassion of all. There is also a time for firm guidance. I must of course also thank prisoners and ex-prisoners who have helped my understanding. But I have become convinced that reform in prisons can, in the end, come only through the prison officer, who knows far more about prisoners, and will of course remain closer to them, than can a detached observer like myself. Much understanding of the prisoner will be needed, too, for prisons can run only through an alliance of staff and inmate, in which the respect of staff and by staff is upheld and in which it is possible to develop in the prisoner a respect for the law and, through it, of himself and others.

Because the prison system is so important an aspect of society and should be subject to public scrutiny, I believe that what happens within it should not be hidden behind the Official Secrets Act, except for details which cannot be revealed for fear of encouraging escapes through divulging knowledge of security systems. A prisoner's right to anonymity must also be respected; but, when a prisoner agrees, it should be permissible to feature him or her in information about prisons.

Lastly, I wish to thank the editor of *The Times*, William Rees-Mogg, and Louis Heren, my immediate chief, for allowing me to write this book and therefore to draw on experience and knowledge gained while working for the paper.

January 1980 PETER EVANS

Chapter 1
The Crisis Dawns

In the spring and summer of 1979, many anxious hours were spent within the Home Office; a secret contingency plan was being prepared in case the prisons exploded into disorder and possible death.

The ingredients were already there. The dangers had earlier been spelt out dramatically in a letter to Mr Merlyn Rees, Home Secretary in the Labour Government, by the prison governors' branch of the Society of Civil and Public Servants:

> So far we have successfully avoided loss of life during serious disturbances but if the present trend continues there will be a serious loss of control, which has to be quelled by armed intervention by another service. In such circumstances there is a probability of both staff and prisoners being killed.

During the 1970s a wave of protests by prisoners had culminated in riots and disorder in the dispersal prisons – so called because the most dangerous prisoners in the country, including terrorists, are dispersed among other prisoners whose escape would not cause so much alarm. They are held within walls and fences guarded by a formidable array of electronic gadgetry – extra senses for the guards in control rooms watching television screens and for men patrolling under night-time floodlights with fierce, well-trained dogs.

But the governors' warning had been prompted not only by the knowledge of the damage that subversives and psychopaths could do but more immediately by the most serious wave of unrest the prison system had experienced among the uniformed staff, the prison officers whose job it is to maintain the Queen's peace among some of the least peaceable people in the country.

The growth and extent of this crisis in the prisons had been hidden from the public. Visits by journalists were allowed, but criticism was not much welcomed and copy for publication had always to be shown first to the Home Office to ensure that the facts were correct. More than once attempts were made to suppress inconvenient facts (though there has been some relaxation in recent years).

But some signs of greater enlightenment did begin to emerge. For example, an experimental course at Ashwell to try to teach prisoners how to survive in the outside world was being quoted by more imaginative civil servants to show how staff, who were helping to train prisoners, could be given a more positive role. And, as part of a greater freedom now being given to journalists, they no longer had to submit their work for 'checking'.

But was it too late? Was the new policy of improved openness, apparent as evidence of the crisis increased, able to remove some of the stagnation in which the germs of discontent had multiplied?

Mr Roy Jenkins, when Home Secretary, had warned of the dangers that the prison system would face if the population in prison in England and Wales reached 42,000. By March 1980 it had reached 44,800.

The growing disenchantment of prison officers, apparent to anyone who attended their annual conferences, reached the point of serious action in 1978, when officers' protests interrupted regimes in prisons and the work of some courts. Politically, the trouble came at the worst possible time for the Labour Government.

While Mr James Callaghan, the Prime Minister, was keeping his options open over the date of the general election, Mr Merlyn Rees, the Home Secretary, was given the job of trying to damp down trouble in prisons. Its extent was being played down, but the Home Office was out of touch with the real feelings within prisons and the national executive of the Prison Officers' Association had not the power to control them. To some in the Government, at least, it seemed best to meet prison officers' pay demands to keep them quiet, but the demands multiplied and resistance in the Home Office to meeting them grew.

Dissidents from prisons in the Midlands and the South painfully expressed their anger at the reaction to various pay claims and other grievances at a meeting in a prison officers' club; but not all prisons were represented. A steering group was established to co-ordinate action. Their anger was painful because they were conscious that taking action had always been a last resort. It was they who had the responsibility of keeping the peace, but now the peacekeepers found themselves in a conflict. They had been put on the defensive by the low esteem in which they felt they were regarded, and they tended, as a result, to see issues in stark terms from their own point of view – what was just and unjust in behaviour towards them, what was right and what was wrong about it, who was on their side and who was not. Pay became a substitute in many minds for job satisfaction and pay demands a symptom of deeper malaise.

The prison officers felt their service to be under attack from within the Home Office and from without, via the organisations supporting prisoners' rights, who did not see that, because the prison officer has most contact with the prisoner, true reform in prison can in the end be achieved only with the prison officer's help. New penological methods, which tend to circumvent the part played by prison officers, left them confused and angry about their diminished role.

Were they to be managers? Were they to behave like the Civil Service, with whose pay scales theirs was linked? Or were they to be para-military? Different authorities expected different things at different times, although the aftermath of the Hull riot eventually began swinging opinion to the need for greater discipline, not less, and a consequent ability to act cohesively with strength, but also with restraint, in answer to commands from people trained to take charge; the alternative would be confusion at best, anarchy and disorder at worst.

The dilemma of how to use strength with restraint became even more vivid after the prison authorities had used so-called 'MUFTI' ('Minimum use of force tactical intervention') teams at Wormwood Scrubs on 31 August 1979. Fifty-four prisoners and eleven officers were injured during the incident. Attempts to silence two voluntary workers in the prison from speaking out about what happened failed, and strong protests from Labour MPs, penal reformers and prisoners' families helped to awaken public concern. Pressure grew for a more open investigation than the one being conducted by Mr Keith Gibson, the Prison Department's South-East Regional Director.

In late February, 1980, Mr Gibson wrote to Mr William Whitelaw, the Home Secretary, saying that he was unable to make progress with his investigations into this incident, as prima facie evidence had emerged of criminal assaults by officers on prisoners which should properly be investigated by the police. Mr Whitelaw announced in a written answer, on February 28, to Parliamentary questions that he was asking Scotland Yard to investigate.

But he said that Mr Gibson would report to him on the basis of inquiries he had already made on other aspects of the incident. Mr Whitelaw added that he endorsed Mr Gibson's conclusion that the deployment of 'MUFTI' teams to regain control of 'D' wing was fully justified and that prison officers must continue to be trained and equipped to deal with acts of concerted indiscipline by inmates.

Critics of the tactics remained unconvinced, however. The issue had become one of double concern, since police had earlier investigated prison officers at Hull (see Chapter 8), and was symptomatic of dangerous tensions within the prison system.

The sum total of frustrations, large and small, felt by staff and prisoners, contributed to the crisis. Later, there was a disturbance at Gartree, one of the dispersal prisons, over the nature of the medical treatment of sick prisoners there, deficiencies which had earlier been described in an article in *The Times*. But the blame at Gartree was pointed in the wrong direction – at the medical officer, who, when interviewed some time before, had shown himself to be a conscientious, caring man. The real fault lay with those in positions of high power who had done too little to remove from prisons people who ought to have been treated in National Health Service hospitals. Too seldom, unfortunately, can the hospitals take them, and there have also been objections by some union members.

It is dangerously facile to see these tensions only in terms of conspiracy theories, as both civil servants in the Home Office and prison staff have tended to do over the years. Prison officers at an annual conference of the Association complained about being treated as chess pieces by the Home Office, which denied that this was so. And some civil servants have in return tended to look for evidence of subversion or have wrongly explained individuals' motives in terms of personal ambition within the Prison Officers' Association. Some of the more authoritarian of state servants would blame newspapers for making the forthcoming crisis worse by writing about it, instead of understanding that in a free society facts must be brought into the open for public scrutiny, not least so that prisons can obtain greater political priority.

There is nothing new in a tendency to see upheavals in terms of individuals rather than the forces to which they respond. 'The perennial excuse that everything that is wrong is the fault of a few "false counsellors" or a single leader has been a source of confusion throughout the ages,' Richard Friedenthal has written in his life of Luther.

The true origins of the clash of views over the running of prisons lie, however, in the development of the 'welfare state', which led to increasing bureaucratic intervention to cater for the needs of the individual. In prison this meant that heavier emphasis was put upon the needs of the prisoner, an emphasis which had begun in the late eighteenth century with scientific exploration of the nature of the criminal in relation to his treatment by society. In 1932 Dr G. W. Pailthorpe wrote that Beccaria in 1755 and Bentham, in England, in 1792 pointed out that the criminal is an offender against society rather than, as had hitherto been thought, an offender against God. Punishment, they maintained, should be meted out as a deterrent, not as a vengeance. Criminals were normal people who had succumbed to temptation. Others later added that some criminals were lunatics and as such were in need not so much of moral training as of scientific study and treatment.

Dr Pailthorpe, a pioneer researcher, described how Lambroso, in 1876, in his *Crime, its Causes and Remedies*, had emphasised the importance of apportioning penalties not according to the offence but according to the offender. Thus was born the idea that treatment should be applied to the needs of the offender – an idea which today still causes fierce opposition from hard-liners in the law-and-order lobby, who argue that society's needs are paramount and call for offenders to be punished and deterred rather than 'treated'.

Dr M. Hamblin Smith, of Birmingham Prison, wrote in a preface to Dr Pailthorpe's own book, *What we put in prison* : 'We see that certain offenders are properly to be regarded as sick persons, needing treatment as much as do the psycho-neurotic patients . . . It is hoped that the time will come when a trained psychologist will be attached to every court in the country.' Dr Hamblin Smith also foresaw a need for psychological investigation to provide means of deciding with what remedial measures probation should be combined.*

Present-day argument about treatment of delinquents is at its fiercest over the handling of children and young people. Reforms during the nineteenth and twentieth centuries had taken into account the view of the Gladstone Committee of 1895, endorsed by the Children's Act of 1908. Implicit also in the 1908 Children's Act was the idea that children in trouble were the victims of society and of their poverty, rather than perpetrators of evil actions. That Act established juvenile courts especially to deal with children in trouble. It also charged juvenile courts with a responsibility for the neglected rather than the naughty children who had committed crime. In 1927 a Home Office Department Committee concluded that 'there is little or no difference in character and needs between the neglected and the delinquent child'.

The furthermost shore reached by all these related ideas was the 1969 Children and Young Persons Act. Mr James Callaghan, then Home Secretary, introducing the Bill, said that one of its aims was to keep out of the courts 'all those children who will benefit as much, or more, from other forms of treatment, as they will by going to court'.

The Conservatives, on coming to power in 1970, announced that they would not implement certain key sections of the Act. 'One of the most serious general accusations against the way the Act is operating at present', write Marcel Berlins and Geoffrey Wansell in *Caught in the Act* 'is that children under the age of 17 are now able to commit almost any kind of crime with impunity. The law has, as a result, been made almost irrelevant and an object of mockery among young offenders.'

*Dr Hamblin Smith described how Dr Pailthorpe studied the woman offender by working with him at Birmingham Prison in 1922–3. Then, with a Medical Research Council grant, she spent four years on research at Holloway Prison and later extended her research to reformatory institutions.

That criticism is balanced by a comment from Mr Brian Roycroft, the Director of Social Services for Newcastle-upon-Tyne, who had summarised the social workers' attitude in an article in *The Magistrate*:

> I believe we are getting a new breed of social workers with a tremendous commitment to their work and to reaching into the basic roots of social ills to cure them.

He warned magistrates that they should not be

> . . . misled into thinking that social workers see the soft answer to all problems and are always against authority in favour of the underdog. Social workers are not, as is often believed, against punishment. They are in favour of punishment for young offenders if it is a constructive part of a plan which will help the young person come to terms with himself and his surroundings.
>
> They are not against taking children away from their homes if by doing so they stand a better chance of relieving tensions, of creating new and better relationships, and of helping the young person to learn about himself and his powers of self-control. Social workers are not in favour of young people committing offences and continuing to commit offences in the community because this is not only wrong in itself, but pushes the young person further along the road of social isolation.

Juvenile court magistrates had blamed at least part of the Act's failure on its taking away their power to make an order to send a child to an approved school: 'Many children who should be in a residential institution are left free to commit further offences, because, as the magistrates allege, the only order the court can effectively make is one placing the child into the care of the local authority'. Berlins and Wansell continue in *Caught in the Act*:

> Magistrates claim that the 'soft approach' of the social service departments of the local authorities means that children who have committed offences and would have before the Act been sent to approved schools are being sent back to their own homes

and their own environment where they continue to present a potential danger to society by committing further offences.

Even where the local authority sent the child to a residential home . . ., he was able to run away with ease and commit further offences with no fear of any more severe action being taken against him.

One of the main recent charges made against the scientific approach, however, is that in the last ten years it has brought reaction, and helped to cause strife, within the organisations representing the three law enforcement agencies – probation officers, police, and prison officers. Another reason for the crisis of identity felt by these organisations is, of course, pressure on members resulting from extra demands made upon them by the growth of crime and a consequent increase in numbers of personnel needed to deal with it.

The National Association of Probation Officers has been split over whether its primary role is that of welfare or to be 'screws on wheels', as one put it. Different officers question whether they should give priority to the needs of their client or to law enforcement through the courts. The Probation Service began as court missionaries, though today many of the younger and more radical members would put the needs of their clients first and regard themselves primarily as social workers.

The police, though involved through their juvenile bureaux in dealing with children in trouble, have in their ranks officers who bitterly complain that weakness in dealing with juveniles is creating a crime-ridden generation. Some have called social workers 'mini-skirted wonders'. The service is split between those who see it having a social work role in an attempt to prevent crime and those who believe its main task is catching criminals so that they can be punished.

Prison officers have debated long and earnestly about how to fulfil a rehabilitative role within prisons, which involves the flexible understanding of prisoners and consideration of their needs, rather than maintaining the rigid hierarchical formalities calculated to win respect (and, among some prisoners, fear of the consequences of being disobedient).

Both police and prison officers, being on average 'conservative', have railed from within their ghettos against the influence of 'academics', 'experts' and 'do-gooders' – a source of grievance to prison officers and police – who lack their own practical experience and who base advice on scientific theory rather than human instincts refined by long experience and understanding. What annoys these officers most is the lobbying power of the outside expert; and it is true that the Home Office has learnt to depend upon the research done world-wide into penological matters and filtered through sceptical minds in British universities. That is the natural development of the first search for rational inquiry into crime in the eighteenth century.

But the tide of liberal enlightenment which is embodied in the Children and Young Persons Act of 1969 is now, apparently, receding. At the time of writing, Mr William Whitelaw, the Home Secretary, is about to introduce 'short, sharp shocks' as an experiment in two detention centres, though research evidence pulled together within the Home Office has suggested that harsher punishments will not be more effective than the strict regime which already exists.

It is against the totality of this wide background that the protests of prison staff must be seen.

The academic world and the thinking people who have formed an honourable tradition of concern about prisons have provided a formidable lobby for new approaches to custody. But in so glittering a display of the intelligentsia, the virtues of the prison officer did not seem to shine very brightly. The mistake was not to give ordinary common sense and fair-mindedness greater recognition as a basis for dealing with prisoners. No theory can survive if it is not practical, or if the staff do not see it as right and proper policy.

The last chapter in this book looks at ways of harnessing the good will of staff rather than provoking their ill will. Earlier chapters describe how pressures built up within the prison system until crisis point was reached. The book will also explain how Mr Rees set up the Committee of Inquiry on 17 November 1978, giving it a deadline of March 1979, which it did not meet; but temporarily it damped down unrest during a general election campaign in which law and order was an important issue.

As details of contingency planning in the Home Office emerged after publication of the May Committee Report on 31 October 1979 and the prison staffs showed themselves to be still dissatisfied in spite of its recommendations, it would have been a mistake not to remember what was good about the United Kingdom Prison Service. Indeed, some of its virtues have become some of its faults: its uncomplaining willingness in the past to accept more people – and more difficult people – than it could properly handle, and, as we shall see later in the book, the seduction of some of its top administrators and Government Ministers in the past by philosophies that were not always strictly relevant or were too generally applied. Those seduced did not always see that, although there are good ideas worth implementing, some of them are good only for some of the prisoners some of the time. Other prisoners need a different approach.

But awareness of what prison officers have to offer should not mean a consequent disenchantment with the often brilliant research done by academics or the role of the Advisory Council on the Penal System: their work, much of it to be admired, merely needs to be channelled through the filter of more worldly practical experience. As an analogy, it is no use a design team producing a military aircraft with dazzling performance if, in the end, it is so difficult to fly that it causes a greater casualty list among your country's pilots than it would among the enemy's. The real test is whether new ideas in penology are as applicable to this country as, say, to the United States, whence so much good and bad has come in the past.

Public opinion has to be borne in mind, partly because there is a tradition since Saxon times of the involvement of the people in law enforcement, which, for example, makes ours the 'police of the people' rather than the 'police of the prince', as has been the case in some other European countries. A too harsh penal system, which was wildly out of touch with public opinion, could be regarded as repressive; or, if it were too weak, people might be encouraged to take the law too much into their own hands, as has already been threatened in Britain when racial minorities, under attack and distrustful of police, have stated an intention to form vigilante groups. It is for this reason that I favour more involvement of the public in the oversight of prisons, instead of the appointment of a prisons ombudsman, which would be too bureaucratic a solution. In Denmark, for example, a reaction against the bureaucracy and the high taxes necessary to sustain the welfare state has had a considerable political effect, including the formation of a strong new Parliamentary party.

Besides, prisons cannot be considered in isolation. Although this book focuses on them, it should be constantly borne in mind that penal reform involves first and foremost the reduction of the use of imprisonment to the minimum compatible with protection of the public, and that informed observers are unanimous that in the United Kingdom the prison population is substantially above that minimum. This is both because petty offenders are sent to prison who should not be, and because the average length of sentences is excessive.

As usual, the question of how prisons are run has two sides: firm and enlightened management should lead the staff, with consultation, to acceptance of new methods of working and respect for human rights, and give them opportunities to use their skills and demonstrate their human concern. But also the staff should accept that the introduction of new procedures – such as consultation, grievance procedures, inspection and new ways of hearing complaints – which are not slanted either against them or the prisoners would not undermine their authority but enhance it. Cover-ups and other evasions of responsibility are bad for the whole Prison Service because they protect its bad members and cast a slur of suspicion on its good ones.

It is time to sort out more precisely what ideas are worth using and where, and to judge by the experience of our own systems and other people's. The down-to-earth experience and common sense of prison officers will need to be used as a check to the wider swings of penological fashions, which might otherwise continue to swing too fast and too far.

Chapter 2

Overcrowding

The extent of prison overcrowding is a national disgrace.

In 1978, for the first time, as many as 16,000 inmates in some of the most primitive of Britain's prisons were forced to live two or three to a cell which the Victorians built to hold one. They have not even washbasins in their cells, let alone lavatories, and when three men share a space no more than 13 ft by 9 ft by 7 ft it is so cramped that they have to take it in turns to stand up to make beds, wash and shave. There are too few baths in such prisons to encourage a high standard of personal hygiene.

Sometimes prisoners are locked in together for twenty-three hours out of twenty-four, sleeping, smoking, eating, urinating and defecating without privacy in sickening sight, smell and sound of each other. But the government cannot claim ignorance. As long ago as 1970, Mr R. F. Bunker explained in the *Prison Officers' Magazine* how he was on duty in a prison and had to go to a cell to give one of the prisoners there some medicine:

> This inmate was sat up in bed, situated behind the door, reading a book. He was attired in pyjamas; his bedding was clean and tidy and he impressed me as being a clean young man. On the wall above him were a few photographs of his family and it was evident that he had been used to living in decent surroundings.
>
> Adjacent to his bunk was a two-tier bunk occupied by two elderly men. The inmate occupying the top bunk was in bed, fully dressed, complete with shirt, tie and pullover, and smoking a cigarette. It was obvious that he had not washed. The occu-

pant of the lower bunk was reading, and he too was smoking. By the side of his bed there was a chamber pot, full of urine, with matchsticks and sputum floating on the surface. This, to him, was a convenient spittoon and ashtray.

The cell table was covered in a mixture of salt, sugar, breadcrumbs, spilt tea and tobacco butts. The smell in the room was a combination of 'Black Bell' smoke, stale urine and foot rot, and, apart from the corner where the younger man was lying, the cell was in a filthy condition.

As I entered the cell I was compelled to step back on to the landing because of the stench. On the pretext of looking at the cell board, I was able to inhale some fresh air before venturing into the room again. How that young man must have longed for the privacy of a single cell and what mental suffering he must have endured as he lay in these unhygienic surroundings.

In 1978 – eight years later – a governor explained to the House of Commons Expenditure Committee: 'The procedure of slopping out has to be done in cyclical order to provide that the drainage system is not overtaken by events. In other words, it cannot deal with the accumulated effluents collected during the night period.'

Prisons had been put on their guard by what happened in Liverpool in 1971. The sewerage system there was under such pressure that Corporation workers were twice called to clear manholes outside the prison after covers were forced up. The protests of prisoners ought to have been a sign that more drastic action throughout the country's prison system was needed, but it was not taken. Men banged on doors and shouted in protest at conditions, including overcrowding, there was a sit-down strike in the exercise yard, and three prisoners climbed on to the roof. Many prisoners broke windows to allow more air into hot and stuffy cells.

The Prison Department, juggling men round the system, striving to make improvements where it could, has been living from day to day. The prison staff, who have had to withstand morale-breaking pressure, have their work cut out to keep the system operating at all. Breakdown is near.

Far from promising improvements, the Labour government increased the tensions inside by saying in its 1977 White Paper on spending: 'Because of constraints on expenditure, there will be some decline in the conditions of prison life and the state of the buildings.' At the same time, it was officially forecast that the number of persons in custody would continue to rise. Staff began wondering what they had to do to convince the outside world how desperately dangerous conditions were becoming.

Even the concern of top civil servants appointed to head the prison system failed to persuade the Government to shut and replace these penological museums. Mr Eric Wright, Director General of the Prison Service, told the Institute for the Study and Treatment of Delinquency in December 1976 that conditions in ancient local prisons were barely tolerable, despite the refurbishing that the Prison Department had been able to do. Sanitary arrangements were appalling, he said. 'In human terms, this sort of overcrowding is distressing and there is nobody in the prison service, from the Minister to the newest prison officer, who is not aware that a very serious price has to be paid for it. Prisoners pay for it in terms of lack of privacy and staff pay the price in terms of increased stress and strain in their daily work and in the erosion of tolerant relationships between them and the prisoners which are essential for the relaxed control of a prison.'

The biggest scandal is that many of the men subjected to the degrading and inhuman conditions which sometimes exist in local establishments are still innocent in the eyes of the law. They are remanded in custody to await their trial or are detained pending a decision about their deportation. Many of those receiving such shocking treatment will not be sentenced to prison when their case is finally considered by the court. In 1978, 26,562 (51 per cent) out of 52,019 persons remanded in custody did not receive a custodial sentence. Indeed, 1,370 of them were acquitted.

A study by Roy D. King and Rodney Morgan, published in September 1976, showed that unconvicted men in overcrowded Winchester prison spent an average of 21 hours 40 minutes locked in their cells daily. Unless they gave up their right not to work they were kept in cells for longer periods than any convicted men except those undergoing extra punishment. Even if they did work, they were out of their cells only as long as the least privileged convicted prisoner.

The effect on people of such overcrowding is dehumanising. Staff may have time to treat people in the worst prisons only as numbers, try as they will. Some prisons seem to be able to work only like an enormous clockwork mechanism, with the crash of doors signalling the start or end of another empty, mind-numbing day – a hell where people run on time, as they form queues at precise moments for dispatch to different parts of the prison. There is netting between floors of some prisons to forestall suicide attempts. Prisoners' ties are specially made so as to take a strain of only forty pounds in weight. A man's razor blade, issued to him each morning by the prison officer, is taken away again after shaving.

When time and conditions allow, prison staff try to put compatible prisoners together. At first they may like company, but even the best of friends can get on each other's nerves after a time. Tempers are frayed by small things, such as irritating habits, putting down a book too loudly, restless turning in sleep, or the choice of a radio programme that a cell-mate does not like. A prisoner ticking off on a calendar the days left to him of a short sentence may upset a companion who has longer to do. Deprivation of sex adds to tension. Some prisoners do not like putting up photographs of their wives, as they are jealous of another man sharing the only continuous contact they have with someone they love. Imaginations can fester during the long hours inside.

The shared cell may make men bluster to cover up their own inadequacy. One man said: 'In a shared cell, you're all big villains, but by yourself you are facing reality.' A prisoner by himself tends to be more honest and direct in his relationships with staff and may not feel the same need to act big. The *Prison Officers' Magazine* article said:

> Governors and medical officers alike are confronted daily by inmate applications requesting a single cell. It is obvious that their basic application is a request for privacy. I have known men who will purposefully offend against discipline in order that they might receive a governor's award of 'non-association'; the sole reason for their behaviour being the prospect of obtaining some privacy.

Yet so depressing is prison life to some young men that, particularly at first, they are anxious to overcome their loneliness in someone else's company, though, unless staff are alert, that may occasionally lead to homosexual advances.

In the single cell, the prisoner can arrange his few belongings to reflect his personality. Keeping cage-birds is a hobby some prisoners indulge in, following the example of the (so-called) birdman of Alcatraz. A prisoner said: 'If you have the blues at Christmas, you can go into a single cell and bang the door behind you and sleep it off.'

There is evidence that the practice of putting people in a cell together, like so much else that is bad in the Prison Service, developed partly because of excessive secrecy surrounding the system. The first officially available record that more than one man was being put into a cell was the 1947 report of the Commissioner of Prisons. 'In 1946,' it said, 'we talked of overcrowding as a serious problem with a daily average population of some 15,800, little knowing that in 1947 it would reach 17,100 and that in the first few months of 1948 it would have passed 19,500 and appear to be moving inexorably to 20,000.' By March 1980 the population of prisons in England and Wales had reached 44,800, the highest so far recorded.

Writing in the *Prison Service Journal* in April 1971, Mr Brendan O'Friel, then Deputy Governor of Onley Borstal, said: 'The impression given by the reports is that the practice of "threeing up" was not seen as a policy change but as a temporary expedient. As such it was not to be publicised or questioned.'

Mr O'Friel later became Chairman of the Prison and Borstal Governors' branch of the Society of Civil and Public Servants, which says that prison overcrowding did not exist in this century until 1945. From 1945 to 1978 the prison population rose from about 12,000 to 42,000 – a figure which Mr Roy Jenkins, the then Home Secretary, said in 1975 would place the prison system in a state of crisis. Most of the inmates are held in the forty-two establishments built before 1900 and the four built between 1900 and 1939. Many of the rest are held in 40 'temporary' establishments improvised out of army camps, country houses and similar buildings. A small proportion is housed in the twenty-odd new establishments built and opened since 1956. Less than a quarter of the accommodation is twentieth-century purpose-built. Far from keeping pace with the rise in population, successive governments

Overcrowding 17

have been unable to meet the standards, as laid down in the Prison Act as long ago as 1952. Section 14 (1) says: 'The Secretary of State shall satisfy himself from time to time that in every prison sufficient accommodation is provided for all prisoners.'

Present estimates are that in 1980-1 the amount of officially available accommodation in the system will still fall short of the forecast population by 1,719 places. The Prison Department's own annual report admitted in 1978: 'The essential redevelopment of the Victorian estate seemed in 1977 more remote than at any time in the past 30 years. The major pre-occupation of the building and maintenance programme was keeping the existing deteriorating facilities in operation.' The governors said: 'The decision to close down the forward prison building programme as part of the government expenditure cuts is in our view indefensible.'

The system is now in such a state of decay and the backlog of replacing obsolete prisons so great that even if it were possible to replace one every two years, beginning in 1980, the last Victorian prison would not be phased out until 2060.

Life in some of the prisons is in some respects more primitive than even the Victorians intended. Pentonville Prison, London, provides a shameful example of a deterioration in standards. Dr P. J. Hynes, a senior medical officer in the Prison Department, told the House of Commons Expenditure Committee: 'The sanitary arrangements are worse than when the prison was built originally. The prison had a water closet in each cell and wash basin. We have regressed to the stage where we have not water in the cells and no water closet but a recess on the landings.'

Pentonville's Governor, Mr R. E. Adams, told the MPs that overcrowding meant that 'there is much greater pressure on the use of the bathhouse and hot water cannot reach the five landings. . . . Everything takes longer, such as the serving of food, so it is harder to keep meals warm.'

Some of the worst buildings house some of the toughest prisoners. Both Parkhurst, on the Isle of Wight, and Peterhead, in Scotland, should have been demolished years ago, but the government refused to spend money on replacing them. Parkhurst had a Victorian bathhouse and shortage of recreational facilities. Only one of the wings at Peterhead had recreational and bathing facilities purpose-built. A central shower house could hold only twenty-one prisoners at a time.

While long-term prisoners were demonstrating on the roof of Peterhead in August 1979, the Thatcher Government announced a £1-million plan to modernise the prison and remedy 'unsatisfactory' conditions. The prisoners, however, said the plan did not go far enough.

Dartmoor prison, grim, grey and also long overdue for closure, has to continue in being for the foreseeable future. It has been an accepted feature of the Prison Department's forward planning for some years that Dartmoor Prison should be closed as soon as it was possible to dispense with it. A civilian worker who retired from the prison after thirty-four years there had been engaged originally on a temporary basis. It was soon to close, he had been told.

Dartmoor was built to accommodate French prisoners of the Napoleonic wars. American prisoners were also housed there. The local church in Princetown was presented with an east window by the National Society of United States Daughters of 1812 'in memory of American prisoners of war detained in Dartmoor war prison 1781–1815 who helped to build this church'.

David Pallister reported in *The Guardian* on December 5, 1978 how a 22-year-old prisoner who became depressed when he moved to Dartmoor hanged himself in his cell nine days later. Before his transfer on 29 November, the prisoner had petitioned the Home Secretary against the move, asking not to be sent to 'this cold, damp, dismal place, where it is almost impossible for my parents to visit me'. On arrival at Dartmoor, he was given the customary interview by prison medical staff. He told them that he had not been treated for any psychiatric disorders and the prison authorities did not feel obliged to put him under special observation.

The effect on inmates of life in an overcrowded old prison can be shattering. One jailed at Manchester for refusal to pay a fine likened it to an open sewer. Stephen Oldfield in the *Daily Mail* (4 November, 1978) reported him as saying that only if someone locked himself in his garage for $23\frac{1}{2}$ hours a day could he begin to get an inkling of the mind-destroying boredom involved. The atmosphere was so bad, he said, that you could cut it with a knife and there were some real villains inside. 'I can see only too plainly how someone can go inside for something trivial and come out a hardened criminal.'

The way that overcrowding can increase stress was explained to

Overcrowding

the House of Commons Expenditure Committee by Pentonville's Governor. At one stage, 1,250 prisoners had to be crammed into the 801 cells available. 'If when unlocking at 7 a.m. you have two or three men per cell instead of one it not only increases the amount of work an officer has to do, but also the danger.'

Running a prison is in any case an exercise in the balance of power between inmates and staff. Inmates are most conscious of their deprivation of liberty at the time when cells are being opened and shut. Then it is that resentment can boil over; slights, real or imagined, can provoke men to hurl their chamber pots to the floor or their contents over officers.

In some local prisons, like Birmingham's, the overcrowding and demands made on staff mean that too often prisoners are confined to cells twenty-three hours a day. Pressure on the system can mean a delay in the receipt of some of the longer-term prisoners by secure prisons better fitted to hold them. There was, for example, a four-month queue recently for Nottingham prison, which holds medium-term prisoners and some lifers.

So many were crowded into Nottingham prison that conscientious officers complained that they could not get to know them well enough to do their jobs properly. 'Most of them are two to a cell,' Mr J. E. Langdon, one of the Nottingham officers, said in evidence to the Expenditure Committee. 'Obviously, you have not got time to deal with individuals as you would like. If you have fifty men, there is a possibility that you do not see much of the cases of seventeen or eighteen men; they become numbers.'

Because reports by prison officers contribute to dossiers prepared for consideration by the Parole Board, a prisoner's chances of freedom can be influenced by them. Another Nottingham officer, Mr T. Webb, complained in his evidence: 'We have progress reports to do on these people. Because a chap is not a nuisance to you or because he causes you no problems you do not get to know him. He is on your landing, but he is tucked away. When it comes to his progress report, I do not really know him.'

Much effort and ingenuity is expended in trying to fit into the day the basic essentials of life and the few privileges that inmates enjoy. Sometimes even that becomes impossible, as Mr Adams, of Pentonville, told MPs.

The simplest example of overcrowding was a fortnight ago when we had to turn away twenty or thirty visitors because we could not get them in during the time. The visiting times are from 1.30 to 3.30 in the afternoon, and by 3.30 I have to remove my staff from the visiting rooms and put them back on the landings in order that we can serve tea and slop out. That means they [people] are writing to me or complaining to MPs, husbands, wives or whatever. The person is almost certain to petition and that means a tremendous amount of work from a lot of people.

Because overcrowding is worst in local prisons and remand centres, unconvicted prisoners and those serving short sentences are generally worse off physically than others who have graduated to the less crowded but more secure prisons to serve longer sentences for serious crimes, for whom the pressures are associated with the prospect of many years inside. For them psychological survival is the name of the game.

The role of hard-pressed Leeds Prison, for example, is really to receive prisoners, sort them out and pass them on. Sometimes, however, staff would like to keep there a man on short sentence at a time of domestic crisis so that he can be near his family. Overcrowding often makes that impossible. But in Gartree, a top-security prison for long-term inmates, a fit young man told me he was satisfied with his neat cell, which he had to share with no one. 'Better than an overcrowded prison,' he said. The regime is designed to sustain men with long sentences mentally and physically. But even in Gartree prisoners do not have lavatories in their cells, unless they get into real trouble and are sent to the segregation block.

The low political priority given to prisons has meant that there will be no end to slopping out in the foreseeable future in the ancient prisons in which it is now suffered. The evils of overcrowding will remain. And Governments will continue to be the most culpable slum owners in the country.

Chapter 3
The Prisoners

Not only are prisons desperately overcrowded and most of their buildings in urgent need of replacement. They have also been forced to hold increasing numbers of people prone to riot, subversion and violence.

TERRORISM

The prisons of England and Wales contain well over a hundred people convicted and sentenced for offences to do with the troubles in Northern Ireland. No group poses such a well organised threat as does the IRA to the safety of prison staffs – even of their families – and the smooth running of prison life. The murder of prison officials in Northern Ireland is a reminder, if one is necessary, of the test of nerve and resolve that controlling prisons these days entails.

An efficient propaganda machine is prepared and eager to undermine the confidence of prison staffs as part of its subversive goal. An immediate aim is the granting of special status to IRA men as part of their campaign to be treated as prisoners of war.

The challenge these men pose to the professionalism of the service is how to treat them with firmness, fairness and restraint, denying them the martyrdom that can provide a focus for political advantage and imagined justification for acts abhorrent to decent people. Part of the IRA's campaign seems to be an attempt to make British justice appear partial.

Within prison, the IRA create their own network of discipline, designed to overcome any attempt to isolate them and reform them.

Reform for them, in the sense in which it is generally meant, has no meaning. For them it would imply abandonment of the strategy they serve. The gain they want is not material but ideological. For them, Rule 1 of the prison rules is irrelevant. It says: 'The purpose of the training and treatment of convicted prisoners shall be to encourage and assist them to lead a good and useful life.'

The more fanatical they are in support of their cause the more they must believe that serving it is good and useful. The goals of society are not for them. The pressures exerted on them by their fellow terrorists are to sustain them against betrayal in the shape of 'reform'. They know what bloody reward is in store for traitors. And at the back of their minds is the belief that peace in Northern Ireland, if and when it comes, will mean an amnesty for them. Many refuse to believe that they can, or should, be treated as criminals, because courts see the acts they have committed in support of their cause as heinous crimes. The IRA and other extremists believe they are acts of war, no different from Britain's bombing of German cities during the Second World War.

Thus the need for prison authorities to ensure that such prisoners are treated fairly is paramount. Any claims of injustice made by them must be handled impartially. If prison officers have erred, they must be exposed and punished – but on the basis of firm evidence, not propaganda. For the biggest test posed by the IRA and other terrorists is of the values of the system itself, the values their organisation seeks to subvert.

The fanaticism and tortured logic which prompt terrorists to kill are at one extreme of a bizarre variety of the motives of the criminals prisons have to handle. Hanging, abolished in 1965, would have disposed of many of them. Once, paradoxically when the Christian faith was stronger, it was easier to believe that the gallows was merely the gateway to a higher court beyond the grave. Today, death has a greater air of finality, which for some makes the judicial taking of life more abhorrent. There is, as well, more awareness of the fallibility of justice and that executions, by creating martyrs, may be politically counterproductive. The result is an unprecedented test for the prison system: how to deal with the growing numbers of people sentenced to life imprisonment.

LIFE SENTENCES AND PAROLE

On 31 December 1957 there were only 122 persons serving life. By December 1978 the total had risen to 1,426 and by February 29, 1980 to 1,533, including 49 females.

Life imprisonment is the mandatory penalty for murder. For manslaughter and for a number of non-homicidal offences, it is the maximum penalty. Of the present 'lifer' population about 25 per cent are in prison for offences other than murder; and of that 25 per cent less than half were convicted of manslaughter. The rest were convicted of non-homicidal offences, most often rape, arson, grievous bodily harm, buggery and armed robbery (Home Office Criminal Department Records).

A 'life' sentence does not mean, however, that every person will spend all his days in prison. What it does mean is that lifers who are released can be recalled at any time during the rest of their lives.

Most of the prisoners released from life sentences to date were sentenced before 1965, the year the death penalty was abolished. Of those released in the last twenty years, four-fifths were kept in prison for fewer than eleven years and most of those (69 per cent) were in fact released after serving between eight and eleven years. Many of the remaining fifth have stayed in prison for very long periods; four prisoners released in recent years had to serve longer than twenty years. How to deal with people for that length of time in a way that will enable them eventually to cope with a world outside changed beyond their recognition is one of the greatest challenges facing the prison system.

A study by the Home Office Research Unit in October 1979 (*Life Sentence Prisoners*) has shown that men serving life sentences are typically introverted, preoccupied with the past and increasingly institutionalised. They usually experience a marked decline in family relationships and often show less interest in keeping their minds active. The study revealed serious mental disorders among a sample of sixty men at a northern prison who were being detained for twelve or more years. One of them, for example, started his sentence eager for education but became increasingly disturbed – breaking things, stealing, and attempting suicide. Another deteriorated steadily, trying to kill himself in his seventh year. He has no friends or interests and prison staff doubt his ability to survive in the outside world.

Others are frightened of being forgotten and dying in prison, but many are elderly and have few remaining outside contacts. Despite this, some are prepared to spend much of their time fighting 'the system' in one way or another, although they know it will diminish their chances of release. Resistance to prison regulations ranged from passive refusal to comply with them to violence against staff.

Some lifers are not hardened criminals. They are people who have hit too hard, too often, or have gripped too tightly.* Others, however, are dangerous and disruptive. In *Prisons and the Prisoner* the Home Office admits: 'There may be some men who are so dangerous that they will never reach the point where they can safely be released.' Which ones, the Home Office is not saying. The most unsettling feature of a life sentence, once a man is inside, is that he never knows how long he will have to stay there. He and other long-sentence prisoners are not exactly sure what they have to do to get a favourable decision from the Parole Board. One member of staff at a prison housing lifers said the way the parole system worked was cruel. It was like the Grand National, with hopes increasing as fences were cleared, but with the possibility of falling at the last one. Obviously the Board would not release a person thought to be a dangerous risk to society, though even dangerous people serving a finite sentence eventually have to be allowed out.

Many of the prisoners who do not apply for parole opt out because they cannot bear the anguish. Each year, more than 500 prisoners refuse to be considered. Rejection by the Board destroys hopes a prisoner may have built up that he will be accepted back in society. The vivid term in prison jargon used to describe the

---

*You are more likely to be killed by someone you know than by a stranger. In 1977 no fewer than 74 per cent of killers were acquainted with the victim or related to them: the biggest group of all (21 per cent) were either present or past spouses or cohabitants. About half the homicide offences were committed during quarrels or bouts of temper, a proportion which has not much changed in the past decade.

turning down of an application is 'knock-back'. Yet no one tells him why he has been rejected; frustrated, he in turn may come to reject the system.

Parole Board members and officials visiting prisons have been told in no uncertain terms by prisoners and staff that failure to give reasons has meant that prisoners have not known what to do to correct their faults, and rehabilitation attempts have been undermined. Even when they have done everything possible to correct their faults and change their attitudes, sometimes they still do not get parole because of the gravity of their offence – something they cannot do anything about.

In prison, some work off their bitterness in the gymnasium, others relapse into moody non-cooperation and sometimes bloody-mindedness. Cynicism and distrust spread. Prisoners wonder who spoke against them. They sometimes blame their wives or individual officers. Wives blame their prisoner husbands for their failure to get parole.

Though there are undoubted difficulties about giving reasons – some of them might actually make prisoners even angrier – at least they would know where they stood. Prisoners say that they would prefer to know the truth, and staff say that an honest, frank relationship helps the inmate to come to terms with his position. Lord Harris, Chairman of the Parole Board, has said that he does not favour the giving of reasons, however, and the Conservative Government agrees with him.

The present system also encourages cynicism about the courts. One prisoner who had surveyed opinion in his wing said the men there were convinced that judges imposed longer sentences to compensate for the part to be lost through parole. Board officials deny that there is evidence of that and judges serving on the Board have said that it is not true.

SENTENCING

But there certainly has been a growth in the proportion of people received into prison for longer sentences, which some observers feel is the single most important reason for the overcrowding. One calculation suggests that if sentence lengths in England and Wales were similar to those in the Netherlands the average population under sentence could be reduced by as much as a third. In 1913 in England and Wales, the vast bulk of prison sentences imposed were up to two weeks in length – 80,961, compared with only 3,162 in 1975. The range of sentences most favoured by the courts these days is more than five weeks and up to three months.

The Home Office believes *(Prisons and the Prisoner)* that the decrease in use of sentences of a few days or weeks is due to widespread use of alternatives to prison, including fines and probation, and by the allowance of reasonable time to pay fines imposed. Any such decrease in the proportion of shorter prison sentences must automatically increase the proportion of longer ones.* Taken as a proportion of the total number of receptions into prison on sentence, those for sentences of over two years have risen from 6·9 per cent in 1966 to 12·3 per cent in 1976. One additional reason for that is almost certainly the reaction by courts to the increase in violent and serious crime.

The official argument is that the increased length of sentences would have made even more difficulties for overstretched prisons but for the growing use of parole. In 1976, Sir Louis Petch, then the Parole Board's Chairman, said that the average number of people on parole at any one time was equal to the population of six large jails. But a side-effect of parole and the use of alternatives to prison is the exclusion from custody of the more amenable offenders, leaving a harder core of the more intransigent and recalcitrant.

The effect on staff morale of the presence of larger numbers of more intractable people in prison is incalculable, coinciding, as it does, with a loss of faith in the ability of prisons to reform.

A disorienting lack of purpose now exists. The result is confusion of aims, dangerous stagnation and a threat to the idealism which in the past sustained the morale of the service – a morale now undermined. The Advisory Council on the Penal System says in *Sentences of Imprisonment*:

> The rehabilitative principle first coherently argued by Gladstone and developed in the borstal system in the 1920s and '30s had become accepted in the 'training' concept of adult prison regimes

---

*Penal reformers would argue that medium sentences should be reduced proportionately, as happened in the Netherlands.

in the 1940s and '50s. The growth of criminological research in the last 20 years has, however, cast significant doubts upon the ability of custodial regimes to reform those who are subject to them; it is freely admitted that the old paternalistic principle of imposing a rehabilitative regime is neither successful nor socially justifiable. The Gladstone philosophy, which only a few years ago appeared unassailable, now no longer holds sway. The idea of 'humane containment' has grown up to take its place, recognising that the primary task of prisons is safe custody, but that help can be given to prisoners within the normal interaction that occurs in everyday prison life.

The Council went on to say that it endorsed 'this change in philosophy'.

The effect of this crisis of faith has been to undermine the instinctive wish of prison officers to help the prisoners to leave prison as better people with a greater chance of staying out of trouble. For prison officers, too, have a need to live a good and useful life. Humane containment, the philosophy endorsed by the Council, is appropriate more to a zoo than to a prison.

The issue has an importance which goes beyond the question of what prisons are for. There is strong resentment among prison staffs of all levels that they are forced to try and make work the decisions which flow from the advice given by theorists rather than practitioners. Neither serving governors nor officers have been represented on the Council.

DISPERSAL

The most revealing clash between professional opinion and the Council's ideas is the failure of the so-called 'dispersal' policy, evolved to deal with some of the criminals whose escape would either put the public at risk or would cause a big outcry. The argument is about whether to disperse them among less dangerous ones in seven prisons allocated to the purpose (an eighth is now being built) or concentrate them in one or two specially built for the job. Some of the dispersal prisons have experienced the worst riots in recent years; only by luck has no one been killed. After devastation at Hull prison, governors in the Society of Civil and

Public Servants called for an urgent inquiry into the policy of dispersal and the way it was working.

The argument is heightened by the personalities involved. Lord Mountbatten of Burma, solidly supported by the Prison Officers' Association, favoured 'concentration' after making an inquiry (1966) into prison security and a series of embarrassing escapes. One man who got away was George Blake, the spy, who had been sentenced to a total of forty-two years' imprisonment.

Lord Mountbatten said that prisoners should be divided into four categories of risk, the highest, Category A, consisting of those whose escape would be highly dangerous to the public or the police or the security of the state. The lowest Category D, was for people safe to hold in open prisons. In between were prisoners in Category B, for whom slightly less security was deemed necessary than for those in Category A, and Category C, for whom even less was thought to be required. The Labour Government adopted the categorisation scheme with the result that in 1977, for example, there were no escapes of Category A prisoners, 10 of Category B, 48 of Category C and 213 of Category D. In addition, there were 100 escapes from escorts and supervised working parties.

Lord Mountbatten recommended that a new maximum-security prison planned for the Isle of Wight should be built there as soon as possible and called 'Vectis', the old Roman name for Wight. Not more than 120 Category A prisoners should be housed there, he said. If necessary, a second prison would have to be built later.

Two months after the Mountbatten Report, Mr Roy Jenkins, the Home Secretary, asked the Advisory Council on the Penal System to consider the regime for long-term prisoners detained in conditions of maximum security, and to make recommendations. The Council appointed to the task a subcommittee lacking in the practical day-to-day experience which governors and officers have in handling prisoners and making regimes work. It consisted of the Bishop of Exeter, Mr Leo Abse (the Labour MP) and Dr Peter Scott, under the chairmanship of Professor Sir Leon Radzinowicz, of the Cambridge Institute of Criminology.

The subsequent report of the Advisory Council on the Penal System said :

It would be possible to concentrate the most difficult and dangerous prisoners in one small maximum security prison. The alternative is to disperse such prisoners among three or four secure long-term recidivist prisons where the majority would be absorbed into the general population of those prisons, although a minority would from time to time have to be transferred to small segregation units. We have examined these alternatives of concentration and dispersal very carefully, since the choice is by no means an easy one. . . . Our conclusions are:

> There are grave disadvantages for both prisoners and staff in the proposal to concentrate the most difficult and dangerous prisoners in one small expensive maximum security prison: these disadvantages would be greatly increased if that prison were of the design now contemplated;
> we do not believe the solution of concentration meets the long term needs of the prison service, including the need to raise the co-efficient of security of long-term prisons and integrate the custodial and other functions of that service;
> the problem of the satisfactory containment of a small number of violent and disruptive prisoners can best be met by the establishment of small segregation units within larger prisons; concentration would be likely to increase the number of such prisoners over the system as a whole.

The report added that there needed to be a range of secure prisons in the country to meet the new challenges made necessary by future strategy.

Mr Abse was to say later: 'The Mountbatten report was a disaster – putting back penal reforms in this country by a decade. Although Mountbatten may now say it was not his intention, the report led to such an obsession with security that it destroyed, over a large section of our prison system, any hope of constructive and rehabilitative regimes.' (The benefit of those regimes is now given far less credence by experts.)

But Lord Mountbatten was only doing the job set him, with the aid of three assessors: Sir Robert Mark (then Chief Constable of Leicester and later the Metropolitan Police Commissioner); Mr J. R. Granville Bantock, a retired prison governor; and Mr R. J. Lees, Deputy Director of the Royal Aircraft Establishment, Farnborough. Lord Mountbatten's brief was a narrow one: 'to make recommendations for the improvement of prison security'. He can hardly be blamed for doing so. What Mr Abse called an 'obsession with security' while no doubt increased in the Report as a result of Blake's escape was already fairly strong before the Mountbatten Inquiry. The building of a top-security prison for people with long sentences was in the programme put forward by a White Paper on prisons as long ago as 1959 (*Penal Practice in A Changing Society*). A special unit created at Durham to handle recalcitrant, escape-prone prisoners later became a special wing there. The Mountbatten Inquiry, called into being two days after Blake's escape in 1966, said bluntly: 'The conditions in these blocks are such as no country with a record of civilised behaviour ought to tolerate any longer than is absolutely essential as a stop-gap measure.' Lord Mountbatten added: 'There is no really secure prison in existence in this country.'

Lord Mountbatten later felt that his name had been 'grossly misused' in debate about prison security. His real concern was that within a secure perimeter there should be a liberal regime.* The Council, on the other hand, could hardly have foreseen the extent to which dangerous prisoners can terrorise some of the lesser fry among whom they are dispersed and upon whom they can prey.

None of the present dispersal prisons was originally designed to house them. The result has been a need to spend on strengthening them far more money than would have been needed to build Vectis, as suggested by Lord Mountbatten. Not only has it been necessary to improve perimeter security, but the walls between cells were in some cases too thin to prevent riot leaders breaking them down to intimidate prisoners into joining them. During disturbances at Gartree in 1978, water was played on buildings not only to prevent any fire-raising but because of fears that prisoners would break out through walls. The sort of intimidation that can occur was described in the report on the Hull Prison riot by the Chief Inspector of the Prison Service:

> A prisoner came to his [an inmate's] cell at 09.00 to ask whether he was with them. On receiving a negative reply the unknown

*Several of the recommendations Lord Mountbatten made to that end have never been implemented.

prisoner replied: 'We'll be back.' It was, in fact, not until midday that the cell door was broken down. By this time the prisoner was hiding under the bed and heard a voice say: 'He ain't here.' The prisoner left his cell after the intruders had gone away and found refuge in the cell of another prisoner.

A prisoner involved in another incident said:

We then decided to have another go at getting out and take the old 'un with us. I got a box for my budgies. When I got the birds into it it was too late to get through with four other prisoners as they had been spotted and things were being thrown at them from 'D4'. I sat in my cell for a few hours and then tried again. A steel rod was thrown at me missing me by inches. I got another chance when —— brought —— down. He was in a bad way with nerves. I said to try and pass him under the pipe and lower him down. I scrambled through the barricade and the door was opened by two members of staff. They asked me if I was alright and was I coming. I said just give me a minute to catch ——. When they dropped him I caught him and got him through the door.

One of the worst results of the dispersal policy has been that prisoners who were not in Category A have had to be treated in many ways as if they were, because of the more dangerous prisoners dispersed among them. Instead of there being just one or two maximum-security prisons for men in Category A, as Lord Mountbatten envisaged, there are now seven, which have had to be brought up to the necessary level of security. An eighth will be available when construction of the only purpose-built dispersal prison is complete at Low Newton.

Yet Category A men remain relatively few in number. In spite of the increase in violent crime, in 1977 there were only 257 of them in a total population of 25,071 adult male prisoners serving sentence, according to the 1977 prison statistics. In other words, they could in theory still have been housed in two prisons of about the size Lord Mountbatten recommended Vectis and its partner should be, had the policymakers felt it feasible. With Hull unable to hold Category A men during repairs following the riot, their numbers in each of the other dispersal prisons varied between 34 and 57. So great has the crisis in prison become, however, that both the Radzinowicz and Mountbatten recommendations have been overtaken by events. The unforeseen presence of so many IRA men in prison is one of several reasons why the present policy needs to be rethought.

Not all Category A men are troublemakers in prison. George Blake, who would surely have been put into Category A had the policy been in being during his stay, does not appear to have been physically disruptive or bullying while inside. But tough and determined people are included in the category, a third of them terrorists. Most are inside for offences of violence against the person, for robbery, or for violent sexual offences – rapists and the like.

At least the behaviour of many of them is predictable, to the extent that the authorities know that they are liable to react in a certain way given the chance. What makes the prison population so unpredictably explosive is an extra ingredient – the unstable.

Chapter 4
Abnormal Offenders

Grave injustice is being done to hundreds of mentally ill people being held in prisons when what they require is hospital treatment; this is because many hospitals feel they have insufficient resources and safeguards to cope with patients whose mental condition could make them violent. As a result, the Home Office admits (in the *Report on the Work of the Prison Department 1976*): 'It is not possible to provide many of these unfortunates with the medical and nursing care their condition requires while they are in custody.' The word used officially to describe aspects of treatment in prison is 'inhumane'. One of the worst aspects is that there are in prison numbers of people of previously good character whose offences frequently stem from their illness. Many of them, refused admission to psychiatric hospitals, are locked up with one or two other unfortunates in cells built to hold one prisoner, emerging to empty chamber pots every morning. When they are allowed out to exercise, one can see those suffering depression, grey-faced and dull-eyed, lurching along in subdued silence, or a schizophrenic quietly laughing to himself.

One young girl was seen by two different consultant psychiatrists about admission into their hospitals. Two further consultants who knew her were also contacted. All agreed she needed treatment, but suggested admission to a unit other than their own. Instead, she ended up in custody where the medical officer described her case as typical of many.

The failure of the Department of Health and Social Security to take responsibility for such sick people has deeply disturbed the courts. A Crown Court released from custody an eighteen-year-old girl with a mental age of eight, fining her £10. She had been charged in connection with the theft of a bottle containing a few coins and remanded in custody. On a previous prison remand, she had been forcibly tattooed by other prisoners. When the judge set her free he said:

> This is an abysmal state of affairs. Whatever happens, I am not going to send her back to prison. I am horrified that a mountain of civil servants and administrators cannot find her a hospital bed. The failure lies squarely on the Department of Health and Social Security. The fact that I cannot place this girl anywhere is not the fault of this court.

The case is quoted in a report, *A Human Condition*, published by Mind (National Association for Mental Health). It says:

> Of course, there are some abnormal offenders who absolutely require a high-security environment, but if a court of law is prepared on the basis of medical and other evidence to send the offender to a non-secure hospital, that hospital should be prepared to take the risk, unless there is a genuine difference of opinion in a particular case. If, after accepting the offender, the local hospital finds that it cannot cope with him it seems clear that the Department of Health and Social Security should be sympathetic and make every effort to transfer him to a special hospital.

Some, but not all, of the Department of Health's embarrassment arises from good intentions – such as the open-door policies in psychiatric hospitals over the last twenty or more years. The result of a great emphasis on rehabilitation, helped by the increased use of new drugs, has been that many hospitals now have no locked wards. Most of the rest have only one or two, and some of those are locked only occasionally. There has been a swing away from the notion of the asylum, which sheltered many people without hope of early release. The trend is towards treatment in special wards of general hospitals, with the laudable aim of putting psychiatric medicine on a par with other forms. The snag is that prisons are having to take more and more of the sad and the mad who cannot be handled in that way. Their Victorian buildings have become asylums instead, providing basic shelter, warmth and regular food for people who cannot easily find it outside; but prisons have not the resources to treat them in a way a hospital should.

Dr P. J. Hynes, a senior medical officer of the Prison Department, told the Expenditure Committee:

> I think the most difficult problem we have is that of the mentally disordered person, who comes into prison having committed an offence as a result of his mental illness but in our view is not responsible for his acts. He is often convicted because there is no other method of disposal. We are faced with the difficulty of trying to persuade them to accept treatment. Some may be so mentally ill they have no insight into the severity of their illness. We cannot force them to accept treatment but only offer it to them in the hope they will accept the treatment we offer. However, the difficulty we are faced with is in trying to get them into mental hospitals. When the extent of their mental illness is so severe, we think it wrong because we have not got the facilities . . . We have the problem of psychiatric hospitals' acceptance of people who have been before the court . . . There appears to be an almost blanket embargo on people who have committed an offence, despite the fact that they are mentally ill.

Such people drift from prison to doss-house, wander the streets of cities by day, slump on to park benches, often go short of food, can be seen sometimes picking scraps from bins, and huddle, some of them, like bundles of rags under cardboard boxes at night in derelict houses or under railway arches. The bureaucracy that is supposedly there to help them merely baffles some of them; they have not the intelligence or will-power to fill in the forms that would give them relief or to face officialdom. In prison, they do not have to think; they are told what to do and where to do it. Sometimes even the simplest tasks are beyond them. At Leeds prison in 1976, I saw thirty of them, wooden-faced, sitting at the back of a workshop, trying to manage the dipping of pieces of thread, one at a time, into wax for use by more skilled prisoners sewing mail-bags.

Their numbers increase as winter sets in. Three months inside, where they can get warmth, tobacco and food, will see them through the worst of it. A senior member of staff at Leeds said: 'Unless they came here, some would die.'

Along with the open-door policy in hospitals, a succession of changes put pressure on prisons. Reception centres took over the job of pre-war work-houses, many of which were closed. With the passing of the Mental Health Act 1959, many patients who had been compulsorily detained under the provisions of the Mental Deficiency Acts could no longer be legally held and were discharged into the community or discharged themselves, although the means of providing them with continuing care in the community were lacking. There has also been widespread closure of common lodging houses and a reduction in the number of beds provided by voluntary organisations for homeless 'inadequates', though new efforts are now being made to increase the amount of accommodation.

According to the Howard League for Penal Reform, seven out of ten homeless ex-offenders reoffend within two years.

A survey carried out by the Home Office Research Unit among prisoners in the twenty-one prisons in the South-East Region in 1972, based on information in files, suggested that up to a quarter of the prisoners serving sentences of four years or less were mentally disordered or handicapped to some extent. Earlier research by D. J. West indicated that a third of a sample of habitual offenders had a history of severe mental disorder. Probation and after-care witnesses to the Committee on Mentally Abnormal Offenders reckoned that about a third of the population in the local prisons could be described as mentally disordered. But in evidence to the House of Commons Expenditure Committee, Mr R. E. Adams, Governor of Pentonville Prison, said that five per cent of the prison population were having psychiatric treatment.

The estimates depend to some extent on the criteria adopted. Some prisoners – about 600 or 700 – are thought to be so ill as to warrant detention in a hospital under the Mental Health Act. Some of the mentally disordered are highly dangerous. Some sick people kill because 'voices' tell them to. Others commit so-called 'altruistic' murders: an example is the man who, overcome by guilt at not being able to care for his family, loses his sense of proportion and kills them, because to his tormented mind they may seem better out of it. Usually this kind of killer is a depressive. Events may have got on top of him to such an extent that their true significance is distorted. He is often suicidal at the time, though this feeling may leave him after the killing.

Not all illnesses are clear-cut, however, and sometimes they may overlap. Occasionally, a depressive may become more menacing because of paranoid delusions, though this is more often associated with schizophrenia, which sometimes hits the headlines because of the bizarre circumstances of a crime. Paranoia, in which events may be illogically linked to create an imagined plot against the sufferer, can be part of the illness. He may attack in imagined self-defence against someone he believes to be in the plot against him.

The most intractable killers to handle are the psychopaths, who may seem on the surface to be living rationally. The psychopath is often of high IQ, charming, may be a good conversationalist and can deviously and plausibly pretend to behave in the way he thinks society believes he should, while really hiding different tendencies.

If you are a prison doctor, it takes a good deal of self-control to stand your ground reassuring in level tones a man in solitary confinement who is saying repeatedly, his eyes full of hatred: 'I'm going to get you.' One such man did not exercise with others – he was too dangerous for that – but prowled to and fro by himself, watched by five officers. Another had daubed the walls of his cell with excrement. With such sick people, the slightest word out of place can provoke rising anger. In one prison, I sought to strike up a rapport with a short man with unusually broad shoulders who, I thought, would make a good scrum-half. I asked him if he had ever played rugby. He asked why. I told him. Suddenly his anger boiled. He had mistaken the comment for a slur against an imagined deformity.

Not all psychiatrists like the term 'psychopath', believing it to be an imprecise form of labelling that offenders tend to live up to: 'giving a dog a bad name', as the saying goes. As generally understood, psychopaths tend to be callous, self-centred, without a developed sense of right and wrong, and do not worry about the consequences of their actions.

Patients who require treatment under conditions of special security ought, in theory at least, to be in one of the special hospitals, which are run by the National Health Service. They are Broadmoor (at Crowthorne, Berkshire), Rampton (near Retford, Nottinghamshire) and Moss Side (at Maghull, Lancashire). But in practice prisons have to contain many dangerous and unpredictable people for whom the special hospitals cannot find room. They are not restricted to patients who have committed offences.

There has been a scandalous history of official procrastination and neglect about these hospitals. The Parliamentary Estimates Committee reported that its subcommittee had been appalled at the conditions when it visited Broadmoor in 1967–8. Six years later, a preliminary report of the Committee on Mentally Abnormal Offenders, chaired by Lord Butler of Saffron Walden, said: 'Obviously, the position is no better than when the Parliamentary Committee reported.' The Butler Committee expressed itself 'astonished and shocked' at the overcrowding. In some Broadmoor wards, the beds, in rows right across the room, were no more than 18 inches apart. 'In these dormitories, the patients, who are by definition likely to be detained for long periods (although not throughout in the same wards) and are all suffering from mental disorder, can obviously have no privacy, and as there is no cupboard room, they are living out of suitcases.'

In its final report in 1975 the Butler Committee noted that a fourth hospital was being built on land adjoining Moss Side, to take about 400 male patients, mainly ill or psychopathic. The Department expected that the first phase would be completed in 1980, the second about one year later. An advance unit had been opened, which had received 70 patients from Broadmoor. Broadmoor was to be reduced in size to take about 400 male and 100 female patients. That would allow a net increase of about 100 places for male patients.

As Mr P. Atherton, Deputy Governor at Nottingham, said to the Expenditure Committee:

> The Home Office produced figures last year to say there was a high number of men being held in prisons at the present time who should be in some form of secure hospital. For one reason or another these secure hospitals are not able to take them. The problem is going to grow very quickly unless it is resolved in some way.

Sorry as the record is, it is surpassed by the saga of the so-called secure units, to fill what the British Society for the Study of Mental Subnormality has called 'a yawning gap' between the special hospitals and National Health Service hospitals.

The Royal Commission on the Law Relating to Mental Illness and Mental Deficiency, sitting between *1954 and 1957*, reported that dangerous patients should be specially accommodated in a few hospitals having suitable facilities for their treatment and custody, leaving other hospitals free to dispense with restrictive measures to the greatest possible extent.

In *February 1961* a working party on the special hospitals, set up by the then Ministry of Health, recommended that 'regional hospital boards should arrange their psychiatric services so as to ensure that there is a variety of types of hospital unit, including some secure units . . .'. In *July 1961* the Ministry issued a memorandum to Regional Hospital Boards commending the recommendations.

In *July 1974* the Butler Committee's interim report said: 'Not a single secure unit has materialised.' Advocating the provision, 'as a matter of urgency', of secure hospital units in each regional health authority area, Lord Butler's Committee said:

> The courts are experiencing more and more difficulty in dealing with mentally abnormal offenders who need psychiatric treatment but who must be kept in secure conditions. Even where a hospital may be willing to accept such patients, judges are often reluctant to send offenders to 'open door' hospitals because of the ease with which they can abscond and also because of the possibility that if they are found to be unco-operative and therefore untreatable they may soon be discharged into the community. On the other hand these offenders may fail to satisfy the fairly stringent criteria for admission to a special hospital. The result is that the courts may be obliged to impose a prison sentence as the only way out of the dilemma, an unsatisfactory outcome from almost every point of view.

On *21 March 1975* judgment in the Court of Appeal provided three examples of such cases. Lord Justice James, delivering the judgment of the court, supported the Committee's call for secure units.

In *October 1975* the Butler Committee's final report said: 'In the face of the widely acknowledged and urgent need, we have been disturbed to learn that little progress has as yet been made in establishing units, or even in providing temporary arrangements.'

On *19 February 1976* (*The Times* Law Report) Lord Justice Lawton said:

> From time to time in the past decade, judges have been put in the position of having to sentence to prison for life persons who ought clearly to have gone to a mental hospital. Judges took the judicial oath of office to do justice to all men. When they had in the past to send persons to prison because no beds were available in a secure hospital their judicial consciences were strained almost to breaking point. It is hoped that in such cases that kind of problem will never arise again.

On *16 May 1978*, more than twenty years after the Royal Commission forecast a need, evidence was given to MPs that attempts to reduce pressure on the prison system by building regional secure units for mentally disordered offenders had run into severe difficulty. The House of Commons Expenditure Committee was told that their future was uncertain.

The evidence came in a study by Mrs Elizabeth Parker, Assistant Director of the Special Hospitals Research Unit at the Department of Health and Social Security, and Dr Gavin Tennant, Medical Superintendent of St Andrew's Hospital, Northampton. It said: 'In the short term, due to the difficulties in establishing the units, there will be no new alternative for mentally disordered offenders.' In spite of inducements offered by the Department, no regional health authority had yet established a permanent unit.

Even worse was the study's disclosure that in 1976–7 nearly a quarter of the £5·2 million allocated to the provision of secure units had been used by regional health authorities either as general revenue or to offset overspending. Only £351,263 was spent on secure facilities; the rest was carried through to 1977–8.

Because the Butler Committee was 'shocked and astonished' at conditions in special hospitals like Broadmoor, it recommended the creation of stop-gap interim secure units until permanent ones were ready.

In April 1979, the National Association for Mental Health

reported such a serious lack of communication between the Health Department and regional health authorities over the units that the Health Minister had several times listed a Yorkshire interim secure unit that did not exist and another which had remained empty.

Only six of the fourteen health regions in England had interim units at that time. The first regional secure unit was due to open at St Luke's Hospital, Middlesbrough, in 1981. Although it will have thirty beds, sixty are needed in the region, the Association said.

Thus the intention of the Mental Health Act 1959 to protect mentally abnormal offenders from retributive measures and to vest their care in the National Health Service was not being fulfilled. Mrs Parker and Dr Tennant said: 'The courts are giving fewer hospital orders and increasing numbers of mentally abnormal offenders are to be found in the prisons due to the difficulties experienced in obtaining their admission to the National Health Service and special hospitals.'

The DHSS reported to the May Committee that present plans are to provide 1,000 places in regional secure units in a programme the Department expects to be completed by 1985. Meanwhile, a very few regional authorities had set up interim secure units, the Inquiry reported. But the May report added: 'We are, frankly, more than sceptical that a programme which has achieved so little by 1979 will be completed by 1985.'

Part of the difficulty is opposition from unions and local residents. Mrs Parker and Dr Tennant concluded: 'It appears that the present plight of mentally abnormal offenders can best be alleviated by the provision of better and more extensive psychiatric facilities within the penal system itself.'

The trouble is that the Home Office has taken a diametrically opposite view. The result is that two great departments of state are engaged in a demarcation dispute, damaging to the well-being of patients. In evidence to the House of Commons Expenditure Committee, the Home Office said: 'It would not in the department's view be right to attempt to make permanent provision in the prison system for those mentally disordered offenders whose condition warrants their treatment in hospital, but for whom places in local hospitals cannot be found.'

That means, for example, that it has not been official policy to provide hospital officers with the training that would be necessary if the prison system were to take on permanent responsibility for the treatment of the mentally disordered. The Home Office knows that if it does take steps to train officers it will be in a weaker position to persuade the Department of Health and Social Security to assume its proper responsibilities. This leaves conscientious hospital officers in prison in an impossible position, worried about the sort of patient they are now expected to deal with in increasing numbers.

The Prison Officers' Association is rightly concerned about the legal position of hospital officers giving drug treatment to prisoners. Members say that their responsibilities are ill defined and that Prison Department training is inadequate.

The General Nursing Council does not recognise prison hospital officers' training by itself as a nursing qualification. Both the Council and the Royal College of Nursing point out that in hospital the usual rule is that a qualified nurse gives a drug and another acts as a witness. The College said: 'Our policy is that a person caring for a patient should be a properly qualified nurse or in training for a statutory nursing qualification.'

Out of 637 hospital officers in a count taken in 1978 only 15 were state-registered. Another 41 were state-enrolled. Only 8 were registered mental nurses. In addition, 108 full-time and 25 part-time nursing sisters were concentrated in four men's surgical units, nineteen women's establishments and two other male establishments.

Mr John Smith, an officer serving at Leeds prison, told the 1978 annual conference of the Prison Officers' Association that the hospital officer's three months' training only scraped the surface of nursing. The officers were then transferred to a prison hospital on six months' probation, under supervision. 'On completion of this, they are then expected to be capable of performing all duties, duties which, in my submission, a state-registered nurse could not be expected to do, even after a three-year training course and successful completion of examinations. Surely it would be in the interests of the Prison Department, prison staff and inmates to have fully qualified hospital officers,' Mr Smith said.

He added that trained nurses he had spoken to were shocked at the duties hospital officers were expected to carry out. A trained member of staff from one of the special hospitals, which come under the Department of Health, contrasted the three years' training he had been given with the three months' given to a hospital officer. Only at the end of those three years was he permitted to administer drugs. He said: 'Drugs' side-effects might have enormous consequences.'

The worries of the hospital officers have to be seen in the context of the furious controversy that has developed over the use of drugs in prison. Too little is known about it. The Home Office has not collated the relevant statistics, but in January 1980 the Government announced that figures were to be obtained annually. According to the *Guardian* of 24 October 1978, even within the Department no-one has known the full-range of drugs being used, the number of prisoners receiving them, or the quantity being prescribed. Prisoners' fears about treatment given to one of their number has already caused one riot, at Gartree, one of the dispersal prisons.

The Prison Officers' Association branch at Gartree said in a report afterwards that seventy-five of the prisoners were mentally ill and twenty of them so much so that they should have been in Rampton or Broadmoor. The report claims that psychopathic inmates rigged up a potentially lethal electrified trap for the officers, and that rioting prisoners fended off prison officers with the aid of home-made spears, cans of boiling water and hot-plates used as barriers. The Gartree officers demanded that mentally ill or unstable prisoners be removed from the normal prison accommodation and be either sent to specialist hospitals or segregated in a specially built wing.

Not the least of the prison officers' concerns at their annual conference was about the administering of treatment to someone who might not want it or might even resist it, though it might have been prescribed for his own good. The officer from the special hospital said: 'When you put a needle into a person without his consent and, if what I hear is correct, without the written authority of the medical officer, you are committing an assault, and there is no way round that.'

The Home Office, in reply to such fears, quotes the Butler Committee on mentally abnormal offenders:

> Treatment (other than nursing care) should not be imposed on any patient without his consent if he is able to appreciate what is involved. Three exceptions should be allowed: treatment may

be given without such a patient's consent (a) where (not being of a hazardous or irreversible character) it represents the minimum interference with the patient to prevent him from behaving violently or otherwise being a danger to himself or others, or (b) where it is necessary to save the patient's life, or (c) where (not being irreversible) it is necessary to prevent him from deteriorating. Where, by reason of his disability, the patient is unable to appreciate what is involved, despite the help of an explanation in simple terms, the treatment may be given : but special considerations apply to treatment involving irreversible procedures.

What worries hospital officers is how to define in an emergency what is the minimum interference with the patient to prevent him from behaving violently.

The 1978 annual report of the Prison Service says that 1,361 inmates were admitted to National Health Hospitals for in-patient treatment, compared with 1,249 in 1977.

The medical service of the Prison Service remains scandalously under-strength. It should include 70 full-time medical officers and 114 part-time medical officers. At the end of 1978, there were vacancies for 22 full-time and 33 part-time medical officers.

Disturbing evidence given to the May Inquiry showed that, in spite of extra needs, the number of medical officers in prison establishments in England and Wales fell from a peak of $146\frac{1}{2}$ in 1971 to $94\frac{1}{2}$ in 1979 (part-time staff are shown as a half). Meanwhile the prison bureaucracy has flourished. In 1971 there were 1,621 administrators in the executive, clerical and typing grades, compared with $2,026\frac{1}{2}$ in 1979.

The evidence suggests that the prison medical service is unable to cope with the tasks it is set. The inadequacies put extra pressure on staff. The real blame lies with inadequate, muddled leadership from policymakers unable to define a role that the service has the resources to fill, and a failure to equip it to do so.

One effect of this muddle is the controversy over the use of drugs on prisoners. Together with other aspects of medical care in prison it is fuelling the prisoners' rights campaign – a campaign which many officers feel has swung the balance of power away from them, leaving them exposed sometimes to physical danger. Who controls the prisons remains an explosive issue.

Chapter 5

Young People in Custody

The 1978 prison statistics for England and Wales show that no fewer than 75 per cent of youths aged 14–16 who left detention centres in 1975 were reconvicted within two years. For those aged 15–16 who had been in borstal the figure stood at an incredible 85 per cent. The keeping of reconviction rates has been officially abandoned for the community homes which have replaced approved schools. But there is no reason to think that they are enjoying any greater success than their predecessors. Sixty per cent of those released from approved schools in the years 1963–7 were reconvicted.

Overall figures for young male offenders (aged under twenty-one at their time of sentence) have worsened. The reconviction rate of those discharged from borstals, detention centres and prisons in 1975 was 68 per cent – a 3 per cent increase on figures for the previous year and 8 per cent higher than for those discharged in the years 1971–3.

Perhaps one of the most disturbing paragraphs in the whole of the voluminous research devoted to young offenders is one in a searching study of Dover Borstal by Bottoms and McClintock. It stated that the longer an offender was kept in custody the greater were his chances of reconviction. No difference was made by the experimental modification of the regime to fit training more precisely to individuals' needs.

On top of that blow to hopes of reform came a DHSS report by Pat Cawson *(Young Offenders in Care)*, which suggested that youngsters put into residential care are more likely to offend during that time than those placed at home.

Yet the number of young offenders locked away has risen rapidly since 1969. In the eight years up to 1977, the number of juveniles committed to borstal rose from 818 to 1,935 and those committed to detention centres from 2,228 to 5,757 – a much faster increase than the rise in juvenile crime over the same period.

It simply is not true that increasing numbers of juveniles are being kept out of custody and supervised in the community, as advocates of harsher treatment sometimes imply. The opposite is the case. In 1969, 21,652 probation orders were made on juveniles. But in 1977 the number of supervision orders, the modern equivalent, reached only 18,152.

It may be argued – and the Home Office sometimes does – that the children sent to institutions are more likely to reoffend than those who are not because those locked away are locked away precisely because they are a greater risk.

That does not explain, however, why the rise in the numbers of those put away is so great. It is hard to refute the claim by reformers that more youngsters are being locked up than is necessary for the protection of the public. A working party set up by the National Association for the Care and Resettlement of Offenders and chaired by Mr Peter Jay (later to be Ambassador to Washington) estimated that not more than 400 young offenders in any one day in England and Wales present a direct, immediate physical and substantial threat to the personal security of the public. Yet the figure of 400 compares with 12,000 juvenile offenders in institutions in England and Wales daily. In other words, 11,600 are reckoned not to be dangerous enough to be there. Only 400 were said by Mr Jay's working party to need intensive supervision within a secure perimeter.

Support for the finding that a smaller proportion of young offenders need be locked away to protect the public has come in Dartington Social Research Unit's study *Locking up Children*, carried out at the request of the Department of Health and Social Security. The research covered 1,197 boys aged fifteen and sixteen who were admitted to borstals in 1975, most of them persistent offenders against property. The study took into account the sort of personal behaviour patterns that imply a need for them to be in custody – such as persistent absconding, previous violence, arson and sexual assaults. On that basis, only about a third of the boys needed to be put away. The unit's conclusion was that just under 300 places would need to be available at any one time to deal with boys aged under seventeen now in borstal. (That compares with the 1,935 juveniles committed to borstal in 1977).

The idea that only a few need such special treatment is suggested obliquely by the police experience of a small proportion of juveniles having an effect on crime figures out of all proportion to their numbers, by reoffending. The idea gets independent confirmation from research in America by Professor Marvin E. Wolfgang, who followed the careers of no fewer than 10,000 boys in Philadelphia. He found that a small nucleus of recidivists was responsible for two-thirds of the violent offences committed by the young.

The picture that emerges therefore is that too many offenders are being locked away for treatment in institutions which have had very little success (to say the least) in reforming them. That is difficult for prison staff to accept and does nothing to improve their morale. Mr D. Shaw, Governor of Glen Parva Borstal, Leicester, told MPs in May 1978 that by the time most of the young men who were in borstal were thirty they would have disappeared from the criminal statistics.

The question is, however, whether many of them would have disappeared from the statistics if they had never been put in custody but treated outside.

One welcome reform came on 28 Feburary 1979 with new regulations forbidding girls under seventeen to be sent to prisons on remand. At the time about a dozen girls of fifteen and sixteen were being remanded to prison establishments each month. The then government said that the sixty-six secure local authority places available for the girls instead would be enough, especially if the local authorities co-operated properly in their use. Over half of the girls remanded to prison have been likely to receive non-custodial sentences.

About 150 boys at any one time – or about 4,000 a year – are remanded in Prison Department establishments. On past form, something less than a third will eventually receive non-custodial sentences. Between 600 and 700 of the total are under fifteen years old. (It is fair to add that courts sometimes do not afterwards send people into custody because they feel the offender has suffered enough while inside on remand.)

What does appear to be emerging from penological research is a much clearer idea of what an institution can and cannot achieve. As Mr Shaw said: 'You cannot take somebody and give him 42 weeks in borstal and put right 18 or 19 years of neglect, disturbance and deprivation. But over a period of years the purpose of the prison service is to intersperse periods of custody and periods of support in the community and hopefully the former will get fewer and the latter will get longer.'

That statement is worth examining more closely in the light of criminological research. In *Who becomes delinquent?* D. J. West in collaboration with D. P. Farrington investigated the development of delinquency among a normal population of boys living in a crowded, stable, working-class area of London. The boys, who were followed from the age of eight to eighteen, were studied in their primary schools by psychologists, while social workers saw their families and collected information about their backgrounds and home life. About a fifth of the boys became officially convicted delinquents. Dr West said: 'One of the most startling of our findings was the highly significant association between teachers' rating of bad behaviour in class, when boys were still only eight years of age, and subsequent official delinquency.'

He describes the recidivists thus:

> Typically, they are socially and intellectually backward, the product of poor homes and with too many children, and reared by parents whose standards of care, supervision and training are woefully inadequate. Perceived by teachers as difficult, resistive children, they fit uncomfortably into the scholastic system. Their parents have little or no contact with the schools, and display minimal concern about their children's scholastic progress or leisure pursuits. Aggressive and impulsive in temperament, these boys resist the constraints of school, learn poorly, attend badly and leave early. Unattracted by organised activities or by training schemes, they spend their time on the streets and gravitate to unskilled dead-end jobs for the sake of the higher wages offered.

Time and again delinquents fit the pattern Dr West has drawn, though with some notable exceptions. Sometimes the children show frighteningly aggressive instincts at an early age. A six-year-old boy, one of the children who in May 1978 helped to batter to death an 84-year-old woman, was said in juvenile court to have come from a family with a history of violence and seemed to enjoy inflicting pain.

Other examples of horrifying parental neglect were given by Mr James Anderton, Greater Manchester's police chief, in October 1978: A girl of three was found alone in the street at 3 a.m. searching for a lavatory. Her drunken, prostitute mother was found in a nearby car with a client. Another mother ordered her family of eight undernourished children to steal from city stores.

On the same day as Mr Anderton was speaking, Sir David McNee, the Metropolitan Police Commissioner, was stressing the importance of the family as an influence on good or bad upbringing. Fifty-one per cent of indictable offences reported in his force in 1977 were committed by people under the age of twenty-one.

Similar emphasis was put on the influence of the family by Dr Melitta Schmideberg in an article in the *International Journal of Offender Therapy and Comparative Criminology*. She cites the case of a boy of thirteen who, after careful preparation, killed his sister in cold blood. The boy later wrote: 'Children soon learn that . . . being a minor puts them in control of an incredible power, that of excuse and toleration of juvenile deliquency. Delinquency provides excitement, and even in the event he is caught, the delinquent knows that the punishment will not be harsh, and often he considered punishment just another excitement.'

Dr Schmideberg added: 'We are still so accustomed to the standards of past generations (even if we do not adhere to them) that we too easily assume that parental over-severity may cause murder. Yet in the past when children's punishments were infinitely harsher, murders of parents were extremely rare. Children did not dare answer back, had to accept even ill treatment and unjust punishment and owed their parents unquestioning obedience.' Today there has been a relative breakdown of family structure and ideals, and of parental authority.

The appallingly difficult question facing the penal system is how it can hope to replace for delinquents the sort of affection and security that a good home can bring. Increasingly it is becoming appreciated that, if the institutions have failed, the fault must lie outside them too. In the more cohesive society in the years before the Second World War, 60 per cent of young men released from borstal were not reconvicted within three years of being let out – the highest success rate ever achieved.

Not only is there greater pessimism about the ability of borstals and other institutions to reform the young, but the system is suffering from a failure elsewhere to take off its hands large numbers of young people it now holds in custody. The Children and Young Persons Act 1969 gave powers to the Home Secretary to enable him eventually to raise to seventeen the minimum age at which a young person could be committed into Prison Department custody. The intention was that local authority social service departments should provide places in community homes or similar accommodation for all young persons in need of it, including all those involved in criminal proceedings before the courts.

The Home Office survey *Prisons and the Prisoner* commented: 'It is understood that it may be some considerable time before local authorities, who face severe problems of staffing and accommodation, can take responsibility for the younger age group now in penal establishments. The implications for the Prison Department . . . are serious.' The presence of so many young people in their care would 'tie up staff and other resources that are badly needed in other parts of the system'.

As in the case of failure to provide secure places for the mentally disordered outside the penal system, the Department of Health and Social Security must share responsibility. It has the power to sanction borrowing by local authorities and can make direct grants to local authorities for secure accommodation. But much of the blame rests with local authorities.

The NACRO working party's report *Children and Young Persons in Custody* noted:

> At present, children are remanded to prisons and remand centres principally because of the lack of sufficient secure accommodation in community homes. . . . Despite some increase in the amount of secure accommodation supplied by local authorities, a disproportionately greater number of children have been remanded to remand centres and prisons since 1971.

Young People in Custody 51

The Children and Young Persons Act envisaged that central government responsibility for the under-17s would rest almost exclusively with the DHSS. 'This has not proved possible,' says the report. It foresaw that one effect of the current division of responsibility would be to encourage the local authorities to reduce their burden of expenditure by passing difficult children on to the Home Office.

The pressure on the system is being increased by greater use of custody and more youngsters coming before the courts. Whereas fewer than 500 males aged 14–16 were received into custody under sentence in 1955, the 1977 total had rocketed to almost 7,000 – a fourteen fold increase. An increasing proportion of under-16-year-olds are sentenced for each offence group. Between 1971 and 1976, when the rate of increase in youngsters put into custody accelerated rapidly, there was a huge jump in the numbers of those committed for property offences (including theft and burglary) and sexual offences.

The Prison Department's annual report for 1977 indicates that courts are using custodial sentences at an earlier stage than previously. The 14–16-year-olds received into custody for the first time in 1977 for offences against property had on average significantly fewer previous convictions than their counterparts in 1973, the earliest year for which data are available.

The earlier use of custody for boys aged 14–16, combined with their high rates of reconviction after discharge, meant that an increasing proportion of them had been inside before. Of the sentenced males aged 14–16 received into custody in 1977 whose previous history is known, one-fifth had done time. The corresponding proportion in 1973 was one-eighth.

There is in any case a rise in the population of offenders under the age of twenty-one in custody. In the four years up to 1977 the number of young men between the ages of seventeen and twenty-one sentenced to prison rose by nearly 50 per cent. There is not enough room for them all in specialist young prisoner centres, which seek to house those serving longer sentences. Virtually all of those doing less than six months stay in the Victorian-built local prisons or remand centres for the whole of their sentences – another example of the way the worst offenders are, in contrast, treated the best. The Home Office admits in *Prisons and the*

Prisoner that 'conditions in the local prisons are far from ideal'. Young prisoners are 'segregated from those age 21 and over' but only 'as strictly as structural and other conditions permit'. Given the conditions described in Chapter 2, the implications are disturbing.

The Prison Department admits in its annual report for 1978 that the greatest strain on available resources still occurs in the young prisoner system. The daily average population of male young prisoners was 2,330, 6·9 per cent more than the 1977 average of 2,180 and 62·7 per cent more than five years previously. The actual amount of room for them, even by the narrow Home Office criteria, is only 1,525 places – what is known in the official jargon as certified normal accommodation. The result is overcrowding.

The difference between prisons and non-penal forms of institutional accommodation is that prisons have to house whatever numbers are sent to them. Judges do not take kindly to the notion that they should tailor their sentences to the amount of accommodation available, believing that people coming before them should receive the most appropriate rather than the most convenient sentence.

The implication is that it is up to Governments to provide whatever accommodation is required, otherwise courts would be reduced to the judicial equivalent of a travel agency. (Logically, the courts' position is untenable. If no prisons at all had been built at Parliament's behest, courts would have nowhere to imprison people. If there were no detention centres, young people could not be sent there. Thus courts do tailor their sentences to available accommodation, as we have seen with the mentally ill. If all prisons were suddenly and improbably closed, alternative punishments would have to be found.)

A dent has been made in the position of the courts in the case of detention centres. All courts in the country have power to commit to a detention centre in any case where they also have power to impose imprisonment, or would have power to do so but for statutory restrictions on the imprisonment of young offenders. The normal period of detention has been three months, but there is power to award up to six months and nine months exceptionally.

So overcrowded have detention centres become on occasions

that magistrates' courts have been asked to commit an offender to one only after checking with the warden that a place is available. The Home Office says that it will try to find a place somewhere in the system in exceptional cases if the court insists that detention is the only appropriate sentence. More room was created by a decision to increase remission for boys in junior detention centres from one-third to half. Fortunately, most detention centres are relatively new, so they do not suffer from the sort of unsuitability of accommodation to be found in borstals and young prisoner centres. The original intention of detention centres was to pave the way for the abolition of short-term imprisonment for young adults. But there are not enough places to allow that to happen.

On occasions borstals are also overcrowded. At the beginning of 1977, 5,867 trainees were in accommodation supposedly meant for only 5,711. In 1976 the release date of some trainees had to be brought forward to achieve a faster turnover. At one time, Huntercombe Borstal housed 184 trainees in accommodation supposedly provided for only 107.

One effect of overcrowding is a greater difficulty in providing training and supervision. For young people, some young offender establishments can provide some of the misery, injustice, heroes and villains once described in *Tom Brown's Schooldays.* Behind the official façade in most prisons inmates create their own shadowy world – of power struggles; a bartering economy based on possession of desirable objects, including tobacco, that can be used as 'cash'; a code of punishments harsher than any the authorities might impose; and among criminals a master–servant relationship of a kind that the upper classes in the world outside have long forgotten.

In some of the dispersal prisons, the toughest characters, rich from illegal gambling or with power outside to threaten an enemy's family, have serfs to do menial tasks for them or ensure petty privileges, such as a reserving the best seat before the television set. The equivalents in borstal are the 'daddy', the 'cheeser' and the 'joe', who fill sinister, almost medieval roles.

The daddy is the godfather among inmates. He too is always sure of the best seat for television and other players melt away when he wants their table for a game of snooker with a friend. He dominates by superior strength or threat of violence and is anti-staff. His status can sometimes be gauged by the number of joes he has working for him. The joe is a weak, cringing creature, much put upon, often bullied, the butt of all and sundry, and reduced to polishing other people's shoes and other humble duties. The cheeser sucks up to authority too much, in the eyes of his fellow inmates. To be called a cheeser is a form of ostracism. There is more than a suspicion among inmates that cheesers are inclined to 'grass' – that is, inform on them. (For a description of their role, see *Criminals Coming of Age*.)

The best institutions keep the inmate culture under control. For the 14–16-year-old coming into prison there is anyway the possibility of corruption, as well as support and friendship, from older, more experienced inmates in a closed world.

Increasing numbers of 14–16-year-olds who have committed serious crimes have been sentenced under Section 53 of the Children and Young Persons Act 1933. That is the provision under which persons under eighteen are sentenced (under Section 1) for murder and juveniles sentenced to determinate periods of detention for certain other grave crimes.

The Report on the work of the Prison Department for 1978 shows that the 1978 total of 91, the most on record, was 34 per cent higher than the 1977 figure of 68 and 82 per cent more than that of five years before. Of those sentenced in 1978, 12 were convicted of murder and ordered to be detained for an indefinite period. The remaining 80 were sentenced to periods ranging from nine months to ten years and in 8 cases for life.

In their case, the contradictions of sentencing are most obviously damaging. Public abhorrence in the case of certain juvenile killers has brought with it a demand for tougher punishment. Indeed, surveys among children have shown that, if anything they are even more punitive-minded than adults. Yet, if a young boy is put away for 'life' after committing rape and other violence, he never learns to develop a proper relationship with girls, something that might help to keep him out of trouble in the future. All through adolescence, he will be locked up, graduating eventually to an adult prison, without really knowing a girl in any sense of the word. Pornography frequently becomes a substitute, confirming the idea of women as sex objects. He does not get to know the meaning of love. Psychologically he may remain dangerously warped.

The fourteen-year-old in custody can become hooked on life there once he has come to terms with himself and experienced the crisis of remorse, which all but the most callous psychopaths feel. Staff who have learnt to look for signs of it provide privacy in which the child can weep, then use the experience positively, helping him or her to a new life. So keen are staff to 'father' boys that the grown-ups sometimes overcompensate, treating them almost as mascots.

After, say, seven years in one place, a move, at the age of twenty-one or twenty-two, to an adult prison can be shattering. The young man and his friends experience the equivalent of grief. On release, the outside world can be even more frightening, particularly if your family has rejected you, there's no home to go to and the only friends and status you have are inside. Many years after decimal coinage had been introduced, there were young men inside who had never handled it in transactions outside.

When such a boy arrives in prison, it is no use teaching him how to cope with the outside world. He has first to be taught how to cope with prison and use it to improve himself; then how to manage to come to terms with life outside. Education is one aid.

Often prison is trying to do what schools have failed to achieve outside. The raising of the school leaving age and the consequent requirement for the Prison Department to educate more youngsters in its care in the new, higher age group has added to strain on the service. The need for remedial education is intense. At Rochester Borstal I saw boys being taught to read with the aid of pop music, used to provide meaning for the words in their scripts. They also did simple crosswords based on the song. Fourteen per cent of the boys there had a reading age below what is normal for a child aged eight and a half, though the youngest being taught was aged fifteen. Modern methods, according to tutors, can improve a boy's reading age by the equivalent of three or four years in as many months. One boy who could not read at all had his reading age lifted to that of a normal fourteen-year-old in seven months and won an award made to offenders for modern poetry. At the other end of the educational scale, boys were being taught engineering drawing so that they could go on to technical colleges and jobs after leaving. Reformers point out, however, that when young people need compensating education to help them hold down a law-abiding job this should be done in a non-custodial setting, unless there are overriding reasons to the contrary.

Staff in some places go to extraordinary lengths to try and round off a boy's character. In one case, a pretty girl probation assistant helped a boy to overcome his shyness towards the opposite sex by learning how to chat her up so that, when he was released, he could go on with another girl he had arranged to meet via a friendship bureau.

In one respect, asking what is wrong with prison is the wrong question, because prisons by themselves may not be able to put right a lifetime's wrong. It is more appropriate to ask what is wrong with the world outside. Certainly the failure of other authorities to provide accommodation, treatment and education is burdening the prison system so much that it can no longer concentrate properly on those who really need to be there.

Chapter 6

Women in Prison

When the plans were unveiled in October 1970 for the new Holloway Prison, Mrs Joanna Kelley, Assistant Director, Prison Department, said that it would be 'more a training for outside living than an institution in which people are kept in rather an unimaginative manner'.

The new Holloway was to be essentially a hospital, reflecting a review of penal policy for women and girls announced in Parliament in 1968, which took into account the fact that relatively few women were committed to custody and that most of them needed medical or psychiatric treatment. Operations were also to be undertaken there.

On 1 March 1978, the Senior Medical Officer at Holloway said in evidence to the Expenditure Committee: 'The concept that this is a big medical establishment has gone.' What went wrong?

At the time that plans of the new Holloway were being drawn up, the idea that crime could be treated rather like an illness ('on the medical model') was catching the imagination of penologists – it was the latest of a succession of concepts thrust upon ordinary uniformed staff on the landings of Britain's prisons who had the job of putting them into practice. A bit later it was quite common to hear a prisoner saying: 'The trouble with me is I'm suffering from a combination of . . .' He or she would have off by heart an impressive list of penological ailments, unbruising words substituted over the years for those that carried a stigma and somehow made wrongdoing less blameworthy: thus 'offender' was preferred to 'criminal'; 'inmate' to 'prisoner'. The intention of the vocabulary was to avoid labelling a person, because anyone condemned in that way tended to live up to the label. It became fashionable to talk of a prisoner's needs, in almost the way one would when thinking of giving a prescription. Crime was something that could be caught from a blameworthy society. For youngsters, the notion was taken to a more remote conclusion. Courts, where right was likely to be separated more distinctly from wrong, lost influence, as bureaucratic control over sentencing grew. Many magistrates felt that no good would come of it all.

In retrospect, the 'treatment' trend turns out to have been a last little flurry of confidence before the dark age of penological pessimism. Apart from the developing scepticism towards the treatment concept itself, any hope of giving Holloway's sad and sometimes mad (but often not very bad) women the sort of treatment envisaged when plans were drawn up has had to be abandoned. Apart from anything else, there are just too many women in prison.

In March 1978 dismay was being caused by figures emerging from the new Holloway then being built in place of the old fortress prison. On some days 390 women were being crowded into accommodation for only 222 (this figure rose to 420 in late 1979). Dr M. Bull, Holloway's Governor, told MPs: 'The general feeling is . . . it is an overvalued notion that pure medical procedures of any sort have any major contribution to make in treatment of offenders.'

The purely medical needs of the women in Holloway's care remain staggeringly high, though. At least one-third of the people arriving in Holloway have gynaecological and other physical problems. Between half and two-thirds have some sort of personality problem.

Not only is Holloway unable to deal in the way envisaged with the women it receives, but it is possible to argue that most ought not to be there at all. The vast number are in for minor offences. The new Holloway is still only half built. Not until about 1984 will it be able to house its total complement of about 500 prisoners. No one can tell if that accommodation, too, will be overwhelmed or if it will be sufficient, but pessimists, recalling past experience here and in the United States, are saying that the more places are built, the more people will be sent to fill them.

As recently as 1970 the official view was:

It may well be that as the end of the century draws nearer penological progress will result in even fewer or no women at all being given prison sentences. Other forms of penalty will be devised which will reduce the number of women necessarily taken from their homes, which so often ends in permanent disaster and the breakdown of family life.

The courts have so far not been able to justify that hope. Contrary to popular belief, they appear to treat women more harshly than men, though you have to delve into the figures to see how. According to NACRO evidence to the Expenditure Committee, it is statistically true that women offenders are more likey to be cautioned than males. If taken to court they are more likely than males to receive a discharge or a probation/supervision order and less likely to receive a sentence of immediate imprisonment.

But those figures are misleading unless the women's previous convictions are taken into account. For a start, the proportion of women with no previous convictions brought before the courts is about twice that of men. If they were given equal treatment, the proportion of women sentenced to prison who are first offenders would thus be twice as high as for men. But the 1975 figures showed that the proportion of first offenders among those sentenced to prison was five times as high with adult females as with men. Women also got harsher treatment than men in the matter of remands in custody. They were more frequently given a taste of imprisonment when it was not warranted. C. I. Nawby wrote in June 1977 that the proportion of females remanded in prison who were eventually jailed was about half that of males.

Holloway staff have noted (in evidence to the 1977-8 session of the Expenditure Committee) that the response by magistrates to such figures is: 'Of course the reason they do not get custodial sentences is because they have been in custody during the remand period.'

That does not appear to be the whole story. Part of the reason may be the view taken of prisons as asylums, encouraged by the concept that people sent there could be treated. If crime is a disease and people can 'catch it' from the environment and Holloway has the image of being a treatment centre, sending them there would do less harm than it would if Holloway was simply a place of punishment. That is the charitable way of looking at the reason why courts lock up first offenders. It may be, however, that the courts are taking a tougher line than in the recent past.

Whatever the reason, in 1978 in England and Wales there was a daily average of 1,387 women in prison, compared with 1,358 in 1977, 1,282 in 1976 and 1,044 in 1974. The figure of 1,468 was reached in November 1978. The rise is recent. Between 1938 and 1973, the number of females in custody hovered between 800 and 1,000. There were only 1,276 places for the new high 1978 population; and on March 31 1980 there were 1,622 women in custody.

Even allowing for inaccuracies in criminal statistics, it does seem as if crime is one of the male-dominated careers that women are beginning to invade, though they still commit only a fraction of the total number of crimes that are cleared up. Between 1969 and 1977, the number of males found guilty at courts or cautioned in England and Wales rose from 321,056 to 445,152 – roughly a third as many again. But the figures for women just about doubled – from 50,551 to 98,567.

They are more violent than they were, burgle more, rob more, thieve more and commit more criminal damage. Sir Leon Radzinowicz and Joan King point out that in Germany during the last world war, when women did the jobs of men who were away in the forces, their crime rates reached that of the males, but dropped back to normal on the men's return. Among black people in the United States, where women carry heavy responsibilities for the family, the gap in crime between the sexes is narrower than in the case of white people. Among poorer people, the gap between female and male crime rates is narrower than among the prosperous. The rise in female criminality is occurring in many countries.

But Dr Bull told MPs of the Expenditure Committee:

The vast majority of offenders are committing minor offences and the majority of those are theft or handling stolen goods and I think it is something like 60 per cent of the people in prison are here on that sort of charge. There are figures too to suggest that the actual amounts of money involved in their offences are relatively small and on the whole women are petty offenders.

One of the most worrying aspects of female crime is the number of young girls now serving an apprenticeship in it. The rise in crimes committed by boys aged ten and under fourteen was shocking enough in the years 1957 to 1977 – from 2,197 to 3,790 per 100,000 of population. The corresponding rise in crime committed by girls was much, much worse: from 178 per 100,000 to 1,058. The figures are for those found guilty of or cautioned for indictable offences *(Criminal Statistics England and Wales 1977)*. The next age group has borne out the same depressing trend: a massive rise in crime among girls who are aged fourteen and under seventeen from 262 to 1,610 per 100,000 people. The boys' jump was from 2,828 to 7,995.

Numbers of children going through school (and institutions) are expected to drop once the present birth-rate bulge has worked its way through. The question is whether that decline will eventually provide the relief the prison system needs. It would be unwise to count on it. The Home Office forecasters have taken the drop into account in predicting the future population. They conclude that the increase in the number of males aged 14–16 found guilty will not be matched by 'a corresponding increase in custodial disposals'. But we have yet to see the effect of proposals by the Conservative Government.

Imprisoning increased numbers of women may help to produce its own compound interest rate of juvenile crime. Research by C. Gibbs showed that in 1967 35 per cent of women received into Holloway, convicted and unconvicted, had dependent children, though only half of the children normally lived with their mother. The result of imprisoning mothers was nevertheless the separation from them of 1,000 children. Over one-quarter of those had to be taken into care, the rest staying with family or friends.

Yet the Home Office said in 1970:

> It is well known that this sort of dispersal has a traumatic effect on the children and may be a cause of their future delinquency or other forms of instability. . . . It seems to be generally accepted that the younger the child, the deeper may be the effect. Younger children and babies only feel loss, without having all the capacity to understand, accept and overcome their grief.

Apart from the absurdity of the authorities knowingly encouraging future delinquency by the form of punishment chosen, is it morally right that, except where absolutely necessary, the sins of the mothers should be so immediately and powerfully visited upon their children, who may be in a deprived family anyway? They are the equivalent in reverse of what have become known as 'tug-of-love' children, about which courts rightly exercise their concern. These are 'tug-of-love' mothers.

What happens to mothers on remand is even less justifiable. Evidence to MPs from the Prison and Borstal Governors' branch of the Society of Civil and Public Servants said:

> At present, not even new born babies or babies who are being breast fed can be received with their mother on remand. Some of these mothers may subsequently be acquitted or have non-custodial penalties imposed on them, in which case the separation from their babies can be seen as particularly unjust as well as harsh. Once again, the problem is one of resources, i.e. overcrowding and understaffing in the remand centres which receive women. Facilities at present would be grossly inadequate for the proper care of babies. Of course, the more mothers can be kept out of penal establishments, the less these problems will arise. Much recent legislation has been directed toward reducing the number of people in custody generally . . . but it appears unlikely that the mere fact of motherhood could ever be enough in itself to keep a woman out of custody.

The prison system does something towards keeping mothers and children together by the provision of special units at Askham Grange, Holloway and Styal Prisons. A written reply on 11 July 1978 to a parliamentary question by Mr Ron Thomas MP disclosed that 36 convicted prisoners and one remand prisoner had their children with them in prison, and an additional 50 pregnant women were serving custodial sentences. Of the 36 mothers, 13 had been convicted of theft, 8 of burglary, 4 of robbery, 4 of drug offences, 2 of deception and 1 each of conspiracy to defraud, conspiracy to steal, handling stolen goods, criminal damage and wounding.

According to NACRO evidence to the Expenditure Committee,

when women with young babies are sentenced they can go into a mother and baby unit if a place is available, though women who give birth in prison get priority. Children much older than twelve months cannot be catered for at Holloway and Styal, though if a mother is suited for transfer to Askham Grange, an open prison, her child can stay until it is three years old. The alternative is for the child to be looked after by relatives or friends or taken into care.

In the units, the children have little or no contact with men, older children, animals or traffic, so apart from anything else the growth of learning and relationships is stunted. The regimes in the units have been criticised for allowing babies to be fed only every four hours (except for the youngest) and for the way mothers are compelled, after the first five or six weeks, to work away from their children for a total of $4\frac{1}{2}$ hours each day.

Prison can corrupt women as well as men. Some young girls in prison are recruited into a life of prostitution, though many of the women who end up inside are failures in that trade. The most successful know how to keep themselves out of trouble. Professor T. C. N. Gibbens discovered that of women admitted to Holloway who were, or had been, prostitutes, many had a history of mental breakdown, had attempted suicide, were alcoholics, were dependent on drugs, or had a variety of physical disorders, not a few of which antedated prostitution.

And the mixing of convicted and unconvicted women in Holloway has made the job of preventing drug trafficking more difficult.

If Holloway really were a place where those sorts of weaknesses could be treated properly, it might be more appropriate to house such women there. But the air of confusion in the minds of sentencers and staff about what prison is for is reflected in the too many jobs Holloway, with its wide catchment area, is trying its best to do: to be a local prison, to be a training prison for the South-East Region, and to provide medical and psychiatric facilities for women throughout the service.

The demands on its local prison role are so great that dormitories intended to hold four women have contained eight, and cells have held two or even three. The effect is an increase in tension, reflected in figures of offences against prison rules.

The prison statistics for 1978 show that the average number of offences punished per head of the average population in men's closed prisons was 1·20. The equivalent in women's was 3·2. Styal's figure was 3·25, Holloway's 4·10, Pucklechurch's 4·26 and Cookham Wood's 4·75. For female closed borstals, the figure was 6·9. For all male establishments, the figure of offences punished per head of population was 1·3 compared with 3·3 for females.

There ought to be sufficient supervision to counter the effects of the tension caused by too many people, many of them volatile, in too small a space, but staff are overstretched and tired through having to work up to twenty or thirty hours a week overtime, partly through a need to provide escorts for the courts in the large area served by Holloway. Prisoners' tempers are not improved by shortage of association, the period when they can mix together. The second phase of the new prison containing the main association areas has yet to be built. Mostly, prisoners have been getting only half an hour's exercise a day.

The prison governors told MPs:

> There is insufficient secure and semi-secure accommodation, insufficient single room accommodation and overcrowding at all establishments. The only high security accommodation is at Durham, making it impossible to allow a change of location to long serving high security prisoners. All the Borstal provision is in the South East (Essex and Kent). There is no accommodation at all for sentenced inmates in the South West. Inmates are located hundreds of miles away from their home areas, making it difficult, and in many cases, impossible, for them to receive visits from friends and relatives. Contacts with local probation services and social service departments are also made more difficult by distance, and there is no possibility of forging other positive links with inmates' home communities.

But penal reformers, anxious not to encourage the use of custody for inappropriate cases, insist that extra accommodation is not needed, so long as girls are being sent to borstal, for example, because of a lack of probation hostels and other forms of treatment in the community.

What the prisoners think about it all was expressed vividly in a series of articles by Angela Singer in the *Yorkshire Post* in 1976. One said:

> Having my first baby in prison, I'd rather have died. I've been out two years now and I've only just stopped having nightmares.
>
> The whole thing's like a nightmare. It's so unreal, you spend most of your time trying to get back a bit of reality. You have no privacy, no time for thoughts of your own. You are living a charade of trying to live with other women you would not have chosen to live with, it's like a huge stage play and that causes the most terrible tensions.

Chapter 7

Prisoners' Rights

Alongside the enormous changes in the prison population has come mounting attention to prisoners' rights. The old-fashioned hierarchical order in prisons has been weakened by the greater questioning of authority. The effect is a shift in the balance of power away from staff towards prisoners and those campaigning on their behalf. Prison officers tend to see this as one of the causes of the undermining of their morale and greater indiscipline in prisons.

The change did not happen in isolation but coincided with the ferment of protest world-wide which reached its climax in 1968, much of it focused on universities. Along with the protests came a rejection of traditional authority and a demand for more participation by people in decisions that affect them.

Already in 1966 prison protest in Sweden had led to the creation of a new organisation, KRUM, and the holding of a 'parliament of thieves'. Norway followed suit in 1967 with KROM and Finland in 1968 with two new groups, KRIM and a neo-Marxist body. In Denmark in April 1967, psychology students of the University of Copenhagen arranged a 'criminals' week' which sired an 'Association of Humane Criminal Policy' called KRIM.

The influence of the organisations varied. KRUM's most striking achievement was to prevent future massive prison expansion in Sweden modelled on Kumla high-security prison.

In Britain, a prisoners' rights organisation was set up in the summer of 1972, calling itself PROP (Preservation of the Rights of Prisoners). According to PROP's own account of its formation, the idea was conceived on the exercise yard of Dartmoor 'by a small group of prisoners who agreed to do something on their release to help their fellow inmates and to open up to public discussion the whole question of imprisonment'.

About 5,500 prisoners were involved in protest action following a call for a nation-wide strike in Britain's jails. The Home Secretary's firm response was to warn all prisoners in advance that merely to take part in a demonstration made them liable to punishment. He refused any recognition of them as spokesmen for prisoners' rights but was prepared to listen to 'reasonable' penal reform organisations. About 1,000 prisoners were punished for their part in the protests.

PROP's demands included a right to parole (still a privilege), right to appeal to the High Court for refusal of parole, and the establishment of criteria for the granting of parole or refusal to grant it. The public and press should have unimpeded access to prisons, PROP said. Prisoners should be in jails near their homes, they should be properly prepared for discharge, and Rule 1 (that they should be trained to lead a good and useful life) should be implemented. All criminal records should be expunged within five years of discharge from prison.

Some of the demands merely took a more extreme and militant form of what other penal reformers were calling for. Some of these reformers felt anyway that the system of granting parole should be more on the lines of a court hearing, with an opportunity for appeal. Others thought that parole should be done away with and replaced by a more refined system of remission. The argument in favour of the change was that the prisoner would know better how long he could expect to serve, provided he behaved, thus reducing his sense of uncertainty and dangerous frustration; moreover, interference by the executive in the decision of the court and erosion thereby of its independence would be curbed. As for the expunging of records, the new Rehabilitation of Offenders Act went part of the way towards that goal. (After a number of years, which varies according to the sentence, the sentence is considered as 'spent', which means that it need not be referred to when filling in, say, an insurance form. But applications for some professions and occupations are exempt from the Act.)

The authorities' official reaction to PROP's uncompromising demands was predictable. They were seen in terms of a power struggle. The granting of any recognition to PROP would have swung the balance in the prisoners' favour, reduced the authority of staff, and slackened their control. There were also official misgivings about PROP's political aims: 'The function of the prison system can only be understood if we recognise the class structure of our society and see the penal system as designed to maintain that system.'

Subsequently PROP became more sophisticated and broadly based in its campaigning. After the riot at Hull PROP mounted its own four-day public inquiry at the Conway Hall, London, to investigate allegations of large-scale retaliation by staff against prisoners and their belongings. The Home Office's failure to examine the allegations properly gave PROP and other organisations, like Radical Alternatives to Prison, a free propaganda gift. PROP's inquiry committee was headed by respectable figures like John Platts-Mills QC and included among its members Mary Tyler, the school teacher imprisoned in India for five and a half years without trial; Dr Albie Sachs, interned and then deported by South Africa, who had become a lecturer in law at Southampton University; Mike Cooley, past president of the AUEW (TASS) and editor of *Combine News*; and Mgr Bruce Kent, chairman of War on Want. Mgr Kent, Mary Tyler and John Platts-Mills are supporters of PROP. Another supporter, Dr Tony Whitehead, who is consultant psychiatrist at the Bevendean Hospital, Brighton, is chairman of PROP's 'Medical committee against the abuse of prisoners by drugging'. The committee collects evidence on the use of drugs in prison and monitors it. The committee also wants a medical service for prisoners free from Home Office interference and control, under the auspices of the local area health authority. Another member of the committee is Victor Fainberg, the Russian *émigré*, who spent five years in a Soviet psychiatric hospital, when he was told that his 'disease was dissent'. He, too, is one of PROP's supporters.

CONTROL

At the heart of PROP's demands is the way that the authorities exercise control over prisoners. The authorities fear that control is already being undermined. So great are the pressures on the prison system that top civil servants have made no secret of their concern that it could break down. Two of the most explosive issues of recent years have had to do with control: the use of a control unit to house 'thoroughly intractable trouble-makers' and the use of drugs.

In Sweden, KRUM successfully campaigned against the expansion of top-security prisons, as we have seen. In Britain, they are a natural focus for trouble, containing as they do terrorists, psychopaths and some of the most subversive criminals in the system.

After widespread disturbances in 1972, Mr Robert Carr, then Home Secretary, announced the result of a review of 'ways and means of improving our facilities and techniques for containing violent and dangerous men in prison'. But he rejected the argument of the Prison Officers' Association that there must be a reversal of policy over dispersal of high-security prisoners. He said: 'To put all troublesome and dangerous prisoners in one prison would be to create a time-bomb and a constant danger to the staff who had to deal with them.' Events were later to suggest that the Home Office had allowed to develop not one but a whole series of time-bombs in the shape of the dispersal prisons.

Part of Mr Carr's answer was to create 'segregation units in all the existing dispersal prisons'. The official report of the inquiry into the Hull prison troubles defines a segregation unit as follows:

> accommodation in a dispersal prison consisting either of a wing or of a group of cells isolated from or, at least, separated from the main prison accommodation. The unit is used for the location of prisoners under punishment and those requiring removal from association with other prisoners under Rule 43 of the prison rules. In the unit there will be one or more
> *Special cells*
> Cells without furniture and fittings used to accommodate recalcitrant prisoners.
> *Reinforced cells*
> The walls, floors and window bars are strengthened to accommodate Category A prisoners.

Rule 43 of the Prison Rules, 1964, as amended states:—

> '(1) Where it appears desirable, for the maintenance of good order or discipline or in his own interests that a prisoner should not associate with other prisoners, either generally or for particular purposes, the governor may arrange for the

prisoner's removal from association accordingly.

(2) A prisoner shall not be removed under this Rule for a period of more than 24 hours without the authority of a member of the Board of Visitors, or of the Secretary of State. An Authority given under this paragraph shall be for a period not exceeding one month, but may be renewed from month to month.

(3) The Governor may arrange at his discretion for such a prisoner as aforesaid to resume association with other prisoners, and shall do so if in any case the Medical Officer so advises on medical grounds.

The segregation unit is, in effect, a prison within a prison. Given the number of highly dangerous and subversive people now in the system, there is a need to remove them from the company of other prisoners if they actively incite trouble. Whether or not the right people are being sent there for adequate reasons and treated properly there is a different but equally important matter.

Control units went a stage further, however. Intended to give temporary relief to the dispersal prisons, their whole ethos was questioned. The purpose of the units was to impose a strict regime for intractable and disruptive prisoners 'who showed by their repeated behaviour that they were determined not to co-operate with the normal training regime'. The original regulations about control units said that there was to be a first stage of a 180-day regime with separation from other prisoners, then a second stage of 'associated regime' in which there would be a measure of 'activity' with other prisoners in the unit. 'Activity' meant work, education and leisure time. If the prisoner failed to work or attempted to cause trouble, he would revert to the first stage and be required to start at the beginning again, so as to complete a further three months of good behaviour before qualifying for the second stage.

But Mr Roy Jenkins announced in a written answer on 14 November 1974 that the existing regulations provided that a prisoner who misbehaved should automatically recommence the prescribed period in the control unit, regardless of the time he had already spent there. 'I have decided that this should be modified to give the governor and the Board of Visitors discretion as to the extent to which a prisoner should revert.'

Two control units were planned: one at Wormwood Scrubs and the other at Wakefield. The latter opened in August 1974. It was a belated attempt to swing power back to the authorities, done with extraordinary clumsiness. Penal reformers were angered by the original intention, which, they said, was only partly modified in the face of protests, that any prisoner who misbehaved could start the 180-day regime from 'Day 1' again. That meant, they said, that the experience could be potentially unending for someone unable to conform passively.

After an outcry about the type of regime used in the unit, the Home Secretary announced in March 1975 that the decision to bring into operation the one at Wormwood Scrubs had been deferred indefinitely. In October, he directed that no further prisoners should be allocated to the Wakefield unit, as it had not been used as much as expected and took too many staff and too much scarce accommodation. Only six prisoners had been earmarked for the unit. Since the announcement there has been no control unit. In terms of its own strategy, the Prison Department had suffered a defeat, though a revival of the controversy in May 1979 suggested that the problem of how to deal with the most difficult and intractable prisoners remained. There was sharp reaction by penal reform groups to suggestions by the British Association of Prison Governors in evidence to Mr Justice May's Committee of Inquiry that the units should be brought back.

But the kind of regime the Association suggested for the units was less severe than that established in 1974-5. 'The aim would be to create a unit which was humane and treated the prisoners contained in it reasonably, but in which they would be deprived of the valuable extras which are enjoyed by those serving long sentences in other long-term establishments.' At the same time, the units should provide interesting and useful work for the prisoners.

The Association said: 'The provisions by which cells in local prisons are available for troublesome individuals is laudable, but there will always be a minority who are not impressed by such a temporary transfer.' The Association refers to them as 'anarchists and subversives who delight in either creating physical confrontations with staff who are often less politically aware and may have less experience of penal systems than these people'.

A positive result of the controversy is that it has brought to the fore debate about control in prison. For prison has to contain large numbers of people who are a menace to society, to other people and sometimes, if they are ill, to themselves. People who lack self-control outside prison do not magically gain it once inside. But imposition of the wrong sort of control can do more harm than good. If the system is too authoritarian, prisoners do not have to think for themselves, because others do it for them. This damages their ability to survive in the outside world when they emerge after, perhaps, many years away from it. Even tamed animals cannot survive in the wild without time in which to adjust and learn how to – and some never do. Tamed men and women lack the will and initiative to survive outside in the competitive or bureaucratic jungle. But that does not mean that prison can do without control. Prisoners have to know precisely what is or is not permissible. But they have to be allowed enough freedom for their minds not to atrophy. Crowding people, whether physically or psychologically, can create dangerous tensions. On the other hand, a too permissive regime leaves nobody absolutely sure what is, or is not, to be tolerated. And discipline suffers.

DRUGS

The question of control within prison versus human rights has roused passions over the use of drugs to modify a person's behaviour. The issue has been dramatised by the example of the Soviet Union, where dissidence is seen as something to be treated as abnormal. Within democratic Britain, and especially in the restrictive regime of prison, how far along the road of uncontrolled passion does a person have to go before the use of medicine is justified to quell what in these uneccentric days may be regarded as bizarre or subversive? Or is such a person's response a natural democratic outcry against the scandalous neglect of the prison system by an uncaring society?

To put it at its simplest, a disciplined regime may be unsustainable if prisoners lose self-control because they are mentally disturbed. Someone who is ill may have a distorted view of reality. It was Jung who described the schizophrenic as being a 'dreamer in the world awake'. By that he meant that the real and unreal worlds dissolved into one another to become a living nightmare of haunting fears. In the claustrophobic world of the prison, hysteria can take hold. Rumour-mongers can wreak havoc. Prison is a place where reality can very easily dissolve into unreality.

The Home Office's past obsession with secrecy has not helped. The provision of facts is necessary to the preservation of a sense of reality. Over-secretive officials within the Prison Department, concerned with creating a good impression and anxious to protect ministers from embarrassment, have been reluctant to admit that the system was at fault, and must take a share of the blame for playing into the hands of the propagandists, though governors have now been allowed to answer criticisms more frankly than in the past.

A new dilemma has been created by advances in medicine which have made available a wide range of drugs. Awkward choices have to be made. It is, of course, nonsense to claim, as Home Office apologists sometimes have, that drugs are not used to control people. Anyone who feels tense, nervous and anxious and takes a pill is controlling his tension, nervousness and anxiety – the effects of which, if not controlled, could lead to a bad-tempered household at least and perhaps even to suicide in an extreme case. The argument is not whether drugs are used for control purposes, but whether that control is legitimate. Denials by ministers of the misuse of drugs have not so far quelled criticism. Some of the criticism comes from people who have a vested interest in making prisons difficult to control, but much of it is also levelled by people of integrity, genuinely concerned about human rights. And, to give the prison officers credit, they are concerned about the quality of training given to hospital officers. Much of the difficulty over treatment of the mentally sick in prison has resulted from the reluctance of National Health Service hospitals to take some people who ought not to be in prison at all.

The controversy is bedevilled by fundamental arguments about the nature of medicine: should a person's mental illness be treated physically or should his soul be cured, if not by the priest in the confessional then by the psychiatrist, listening sympathetically at the couch as the patient unburdens himself of guilt and painful imaginings?

Two prisoners at Parkhurst who were aggressive and had strong sexual drives were reported in *The Times* of 15 August 1972 to have had surgery in the centres of the brain associated with feeding, fighting and procreation. One man had murdered a woman. He was said to have lost his aggression while retaining his sexual drive. The other man was an aggressive homosexual, who beat a young man nearly to death. *The Times* reported that he was still homosexual but was said to be not aggressive. Follow-up tests had shown no deterioration at all in other aspects of the men's personalities.

The important difference between brain surgery of that sort and the use of drugs is, of course, that the former is irreversible. The drugs issue is complicated by the fact that prisoners may wish to have drugs when they are not justified. At other times they are. I was present during a group therapy session at Grendon Underwood, the psychiatric prison, which involved a man who had asked for a prescription to defer and soothe away the onset of violence. He had received what is known in prison jargon as a 'Dear John' – a letter from his wife saying she was going to seek a divorce. He asked for a drug to calm him until he could come to terms with the news.

It was a clear example of a prisoner seeking use of a drug to help him control himself. Use of a straitjacket would hardly have been preferable had his request been refused. The issue of drugs used for control purposes was faced honestly in an article in the *Prison Medical Journal* in October 1978 by C. H. McCleery, Medical Officer at Parkhurst Prison.

In it, he described a small pilot study of a drug called Depixol (Flupenthixol deconoate) conducted at Albany Prison. There had been no satisfactory way of containing psychopaths who 'as a result of situational stress' had presented the discipline staff with control problems. The psychopaths concerned resorted to spontaneous outbursts of senseless aggression, inflicting damage to staff, inmates and themselves, as well as to damage to property and, by virtue of their psychopathy, were 'incapable of learning by experience', Dr McCleery said.

The controversy was increased by his statement that 'from a medical angle these men show no evidence of formal mental illness as such'. Yet they were characters 'having a lot of nervous tension, a certain amount of depression, considerable frustration with a low flash-point, who, until the situational stress can be removed or modified, are potentially either very dangerous or, in the case of the more inadequate, an unmitigated nuisance'. The men were considered by the Governor and discipline staff to be medical problems as they did not, or would not, respond to the standard control measures available to them in a maximum-security prison.

The article admitted that 'we lack any local hospitalisation facilities'. Attempts to admit them to Parkhurst hospital were frowned on 'quite understandably', as they were regarded as being purely Albany discipline failures and were not mentally ill. If admitted to Parkhurst they promptly responded as the situational stress had gone. But the same behaviour pattern resumed as soon as they were returned to Albany. 'Up till now we have endeavoured to contain the situation using every ounce of tact and with an umbrella of Valium, Tranzene, Lentizol and Mogadon in some combination.'

Though treatment was useful as a short-term containment, tolerance to the drugs rapidly developed and 'huge doses became necessary which reduce the patient to a "cabbage existence" during which his tolerance level increases' but his powers of rationalisation and concentration diminish.

It was against that background that Dr McCleery chose three aggressive and three inadequate psychopaths for 20 mg 1M Depixol and followed their subsequent progress. Though there were many men in those groups, 'it took a lot of persuasion to get any to agree to have the injections and only six availed themselves for the treatment'.

Five out of six of the men were improved, in Dr McCleery's opinion. 'The treatment enabled us to "buy" a trouble-free period during which these hitherto very troublesome patients were able to readjust themselves and develop constructive and healthy attitudes, thereby improving their parole and subsequent release prospects. Side effects were quite minimal.'

His conclusion: 'Depixol would seem to offer an alternative approach in the short-term management of aggressive psychopathic patients who are proving difficult to control by more conventional methods. It has only limited effect on the non-aggressive patient but has been shown to relieve tension headaches and neurodermatitis and, again, could be worth a trial in such patients when all else fails.'

Another related issue is why the principle of 'C' wing at Parkhurst could not be employed elsewhere in the prison system to handle such people as Dr McCleery describes. The idea of 'C' wing, introduced after a riot, was to contain aggressive and disturbed people in a deliberately relaxed atmosphere, so as to keep tension low. He admits that the prisoners he treated responded to that sort of environment, but once removed from it reacted badly to pressure. That suggests that the treatment was needed more by the prison system than by the prisoners.

Apart from the question of ethics, the problem with prescribing drugs is how to ensure that people considered to be in need of them continue to take them when no longer under direct supervision. Sex offenders who agree to treatment may be given drugs regularly to dampen their abnormal urges. In reply to controversy about Dr McCleery's article, a Home Office spokesman was quoted in *The Guardian* (October 23 1978) as saying that prison doctors never have and never will 'experiment' on prisoners.

And in December 1978 Dr Shirley Summerskill, a junior Home Office minister, told the House of Commons that drugs were prescribed only when prison medical officers judged them to be clinically justified. There was no question of prisoners being forced to use hormones or other drug treatments to control sexual urges. She denied that prisoners were used for the trial of new drugs, like hormone drugs. But Mr Ian Mikardo, Labour MP for Bethnal Green and Bow, said there was enormous evidence that the use of drugs in prisons had increased very rapidly. He had visited many prisoners and had seen bright, intelligent men turned into near zombies. The Home Office ought to come clean, he said.

Pace Mr Mikardo, drugs have also been used increasingly in hospitals outside prisons. Bright, intelligent men can crumple if they are depressed and are not treated with medication. Drugs are widely prescribed to treat such depression; it may be necessary to damp down panics that patients themselves cannot control and put anxious minds at rest until people can react normally once more.

More light is thrown on the use of sex drugs by a story in *The Times* of 10 September 1973: 'Benperidol, a drug which reduces abnormal sexual drive, will be available from today'. It was licensed under the Medicines Act and a 'preliminary trial' on sexual offenders in Britain was reported in *Medicine, Science and the Law* in July 1973.

Dr. L. H. Field, visiting psychotherapist at Wormwood Scrubs Prison, explained how twenty-eight men considered to be intelligent and co-operative were selected. He said: 'Fourteen were serving sentences of imprisonment and fourteen were attending a psychiatric out-patient department following release from prison or as a condition of a probation order.' He added: 'The universal findings were abolition of sexual desire.'

When Dr Harry Masheter, medical director of the manufacturers, Janssen Pharmaceutical Ltd, was asked about the ethics of conducting a trial of the drug on prisoners, he said:

> The drugs had been in use for four years on the continent before the trials here. It is not as if we are doing something dangerous. The drug will undoubtedly give people who would otherwise have been a danger to society and their own well-being a chance to lead normal lives.

One of the advantages claimed for Benperidol was that patients did not develop physical changes, as had happened with some other forms of treatment. One of the other drugs used (not Benperidol) to dampen sexual urges has the effect of enlarging the breasts. An operation is then needed to remove them. The Home Office says that all patients undergoing that form of treatment have been told they could develop breasts as a result.

Accepting Home Office statements that no pressure is being put officially on prisoners to accept treatment, that does not mean, however, that the prisoners do not feel under some form of pressure. For a start, it is pressure, real or imagined, that may make them feel ill in the first place. Part of the task of treatment is to remove the pressure or enable patients to come to terms with it. Some patients take the initiative in asking for drug treatment in the hope that it will relieve them of urges that torment them and thus enable them to live more at peace with themselves or others.

The wish to obtain parole may also be an influence. Even if there is not a stick persuading men to accept drug treatment, how are they to regard the prospect of parole, except as a carrot? In the circumstances, it would be odd if they did not think, rightly or wrongly, that their chances of parole might be increased if they showed themselves eager for treatment, whatever inducements doctors did, or did not, hold out. After all, one of the main criticisms of the way the parole system has been administered up to now is that prisoners are not very sure what they have, or have not, to do to deserve being granted parole. Prisoners are not told the reasons for refusal of parole.

One of the most telling arguments in favour of the use of such drugs is that, if patients respond to them, other forms of control can more easily be done away with. It was because of the possibilities opened up in National Health hospital treatments by the discovery of new forms of drug treatment that doors were opened in the 1950s; one of the present complaints of prison staff is that because the whole thrust of psychiatric treatment has been towards opening doors hospitals are now reluctant to close them on potentially dangerous people for whom secure accommodation is needed. They have to be contained in prison instead.

CONFINEMENT

Physical confinement might be, in some cases, a possible though obnoxious alternative if drugs were not used. *Prisons and the Prisoner* says that the statutory rules authorise temporary confinement in a protected room or in a special sound-proof cell fitted with unbreakable furniture, but not as a punishment, nor for longer than the prisoner's behaviour requires it.

Alternatively, the governor may order a prisoner to be put under restraint where that is necessary to prevent the prisoner from injuring himself or others, damaging property or creating a disturbance. Mechanical restraints may not, however, be used inside a prison either for safe custody or for punishment. What that means can be seen in the Home Office Prison Statistics for 1978.

A loose canvas restraint jacket was used nine times on medical grounds by direction of the medical officer and protected rooms for temporary confinement 142 times. On other grounds, a body belt was used twenty-one times, handcuffs five times and ankle straps twice. Special cells, other than protected rooms, were used 417 times for temporary confinement.

DISCIPLINE

The outside body appointed to keep an eye on the way prisons are run is the Board of Visitors. One board is appointed to each establishment. The secrecy surrounding the system has meant that the efforts boards have made in many cases to safeguard the interests of prisoners, as well as of staff, have not been given the credit they deserved. The boards have been looked upon as 'establishment' bodies, part of the system, and too close to the governor to offer the sort of independent criticism which might have made the world sit up and take proper notice of the deteriorating state of the prisons. Only recently, in evidence to Mr Justice May's Committee, have some made their views public. In the past, other unofficial organisations have made the running with comments which have made the boards seem ineffectual in comparison and put them on the defensive.

Work of the members, who must include a proportion of magistrates, is voluntary. The idea is that they constitute an independent body of representatives of the local community to which any inmate may make a complaint or request, both at their regular meetings (usually held every few weeks) and during the visits, between times, which individual members make.

The boards also have an inspectoral role, with a view to reporting to, and making recommendations to, the Home Secretary on any incompetence or abuse. As the superior disciplinary body of the prison, the board adjudicates when inmates are charged with the more serious offences against discipline.

A more difficult criticism to refute is that the boards' independence is apparently compromised by their role as part of the prison's disciplinary procedures. However much the Prison Department may prefer to keep a bureaucratic blanket over such proceedings, they are being made subject to increasing outside scrutiny.

Thus, the clash of argument which would never have been heard in the silent, solemn, disciplined world of the prison system a few years back, is sounding more loudly, with charges and counter-charges hurled to and fro. No wonder prison officers feel that their authority is not what it was and a defensive Home Office, bereft of ideas, has been so damagingly indecisive in finding a replacement policy of any real credibility.

Prisons were brought more within reach of the legal procedures in the world outside by a decision of the High Court that the correctness of procedure in hearings by boards of visitors could be subject to scrutiny by outside courts. In June 1979, five prisoners involved in the Hull riot, who claimed that they had been denied justice in disciplinary hearings, had part of the findings of the Hull Board of Visitors set aside. Lord Justice Geoffrey Lane ruled that they had not been given a fair hearing of some of the charges against them.

Access to the European Commission on Human Rights has provided another means of securing justice for prisoners. A breakthrough was made with the Knechtl case, involving a prisoner who had to have his leg amputated while inside. Permission to sue the Home Office for negligence was refused and he was denied access to legal advice. The European Commission accepted jurisdiction when he petitioned them, but before the hearing took place a settlement of £750 was agreed with the Home Office. As a result, rules were relaxed in 1972 to enable freer correspondence with legal advisers and access to independent medical opinion, to which a prisoner is party.

Given that prisons remain places where control is exercised in the last resort in a more or less authoritarian manner, prison officers see any enhancement of prisoners' rights as diminishing the authority of those in charge, however much they must depend upon the acquiescence of the prison population to make regimes work. Prison officers have felt more exposed since a ruling by the European Court of Human Rights in Strasbourg (February 1975) on the case of a former prisoner, Mr Sidney Golder.

The court decided that the Home Office had been in breach of the European Convention on Human Rights by its refusal to allow him access to a solicitor, thereby denying him the opportunity to bring an action against a prison officer. The outcome was an announcement by Mr Jenkins, Home Secretary, on 6 August 1975 that, in future, prisoners would be free to seek legal advice about taking civil proceedings without the need first to petition the Secretary of State. They would also be able to take civil action without petitioning, provided that, if the case was about prison administration, the complaint first went through the normal existing channels to give the authorities a chance to provide a remedy.

A finding by the Ombudsman led in 1976 to a further concession by the Prison Department that a prisoner could write about his own health or that of members of his family to a registered medical practitioner by whom he or they have been treated.

The Convention on Human Rights allowed yet another attack to be made on the Home Office position in January 1979, when Commission officials began negotiations with solicitors representing seven prisoners to try to resolve a dispute over censorship. Article 8 of the Convention protects a person's right to 'respect for his correspondence'.

Seven test letters had been ruled admissible by the European Commission on Human Rights. They were addressed to MPs, solicitors and journalists, as well as to family and friends. They dealt with conditions in prisons, civil and criminal proceedings, requests for information, advice or help, business transactions, and family problems, according to the Commission.

In its initial response to the Commission the British Government contended that some of the applicants had not exhausted the internal complaints procedure. In those cases where the procedure had been used unsuccessfully, the government argued that the letters were properly stopped for other reasons, including the discussion of crime, and unjustifiable complaints about the courts and prison authorities. All those reasons, it claimed, were covered by the exception clauses in the convention for 'the prevention of disorder or crime'.

Whatever the rights and wrongs of the latest cases, the impression has generally been left of a Prison Department with no clear strategy for dealing with the advance of human rights in British prisons and doing all it can to argue against some of the fundamental ones being granted. Again, through a too rigid and negative response, the Home Office has given propaganda and credence to its critics.

The issues at stake are the opening up of prisons to a wider scrutiny, so that justice can be seen to be done. They are to do with relating prisons more to what happens in the outside world, so that there is not a double standard; and so that what happens in them is not out of sight and therefore out of mind. It is because prisons were out of mind that they assumed political importance only when Parliament became alarmed by the prospect of imminent disaster. Their worsening plight has not been given the government priority it deserved and only now is beginning to catch the attention of the public.

Chapter 8
Riots

Trouble in the prison system would not have reached such an explosive crisis had Governments been more responsive to criticism about the deterioration of the service.

Official reticence about impending trouble is well illustrated by the way in which a riot at Parkhurst, portent of chaos to come, was blandly dismissed in a six-line paragraph in the Prison Department's annual report for 1969. It was considered to warrant no more space than an account, also in the annual report, of the chaplains' annual retreat and conference.

The paragraph in question, tucked away on page 15 of the report and innocuously headed 'Parkhurst', said:

> On October 24 a serious disturbance occurred at Parkhurst in which a number of prison officers were injured; nine prisoners were subsequently committed for trial (seven were subsequently convicted and sentenced to varying terms of further imprisonment). The special problems posed by the concentration of disturbed and difficult prisoners at Parkhurst are the subject of a continuing study, as a result of which it has been decided, among other measures, to establish a medically-orientated unit in the prison.

Connoisseurs of the nuances of Whitehallese may savour the use of the word 'concentration'. The little paragraph implies that putting disturbed and difficult prisoners together in one place was the reason for the trouble. It was Lord Mountbatten's idea, remember, backed by the practical knowledge of the prison officers, to put together the prisoners who, if they escaped, would cause serious danger to the public. But he wished the regime to be suitable and liberal within a properly secure perimeter, which could allow as much freedom as possible within. The implication of that paragraph was further criticism of the idea of concentration *per se*. At the time dispersal was the 'in' thing, but its weaknesses, as we shall see, were to become devastatingly and expensively apparent.

The Prison Department's coyness was not confined to the annual report. The report of the inquiry into the riot has never been published. Nor has it been properly circulated so that prison staff could benefit from lessons drawn. Astonishingly, the section on publicity in the 1969 annual report did not even mention coverage given to the riot, but instead chided press, radio and television for 'a tendency for greater prominence to be given to stories about individual prisoners, particularly those who have achieved some notoriety, than to developments in penal treatment'.

As we have seen, the treatment philosophy has now lost credibility, and the experts are instead busily wondering what else to recommend. The individual prisoners, particularly those who have achieved some notoriety, have become so restive that the crisis in prisons can no longer be played down. Yet some lack of frankness has persisted. Almost a decade later, the biggest newspaper story about prisons was of prison officers' disruption of work. The annual report of 1977 did not refer to it. The 1978 report remedies that startling omission.

The reluctance of the Prison Department to acknowledge early enough the seriousness of the crisis had contributed to the feelings of frustration of prisoners and staff; the Directors General of the service had in more recent years, in marked contrast with the bureaucratic inertia surrounding them, uttered occasional warnings. The general sense of frustration has helped to fuel outbreaks of trouble.

Ten years after Professor Radzinowicz produced his report, Mr Peter Waugh, then Vice-Chairman of the Prison Officers' Association, told MPs of the Expenditure Committee: 'Nearly every dispersal prison in this country has had a major outbreak of some sort of violence.' Parkhurst, an exceptional prison in terms of the number of abnormal inmates it contains, pioneered protest that has since spread wider than the dispersal prisons; even the annual report was forced to pay more attention, though it continued to chide the media for their interest.

The 1972 annual report said: 'The existence of a substratum of unrest, the encouragement provided by the interest of the media, and the attraction of the relatively untried but currently popular protest form of a sit-down demonstration, tended to sustain something of a chain reaction over a considerable period.'

Had the interest of the media been acted upon instead of being brushed aside, prisons might not be in the sorry mess they are today. For the report showed no interest in possible weaknesses in the way in which prisons were administered – one of the major causes of growing trouble.

Fortunately, there are other accounts of the events leading to the troubles, notably one by Roy King and Kenneth W. Elliott in *Albany: Birth of a Prison – End of an Era*. They say about Albany: 'It is impossible to avoid the conclusion that the dispersal policy was responsible for the massive deterioration in the quality of life between 1969 and 1972.'

The Radzinowicz subcommittee had thought that under the dispersal policy the most difficult and dangerous prisoners would be absorbed into the general population. Where they were not absorbed, the use of Rule 43, to remove disruptive and subversive prisoners to the segregation unit, would provide a safeguard for the continuance of the 'liberal and constructive regime' which the subcommittee wished to see.

King and Elliott comment:

> Albany did disperse its difficult and dangerous prisoners among the general population – a general population that was bewildering in its variety. And it did maintain a liberal regime based on the almost complete freedom of association (between prisoners) from unlock in the morning until lock-up at night. So many problems ensued, however, that even the heaviest reliance on Rule 43 did not contain them. Indeed, it must be obvious that the measures that were eventually introduced in an attempt to solve the problems represented very severe inroads into, if not a complete reversal of, the two main elements in the dispersal policy: the principle of absorbing difficult prisoners and the principle of maintaining a liberal regime.

A series of demonstrations early in May 1972 spread to forty-one prisons in the following months. On 4 August about 22 per cent of the total adult male population in closed prisons demonstrated at one time : 5,500 prisoners in twenty-eight prisons.

At the end of August and the beginning of September 1972, the mood changed. Demonstrations could no longer be counted upon to be passive and orderly. Property was damaged, prisoners climbed on to roofs, missiles were thrown.

At Albany, small fires were started and cell windows and furniture smashed when a group of prisoners demonstrated violently against being confined to their cells for several days. Large-scale escape plans were discovered and kit with which to carry them out. At nearby Parkhurst, prisoners then stayed on the roof for a week and the unrest quickly spread to about a further twenty prisons. Two significant demonstrations followed in November: the first at Albany, when fifteen prisoners still in the segregation unit as a result of their misbehaviour in August barricaded themselves in their cells and caused damage.

At Gartree, another dispersal prison, fourteen prisoners attempted unsuccessfully to escape. Allegations about staff who apprehended them provoked prisoners in two wings to violent and prolonged demonstrations. Twelve officers and five prisoners were injured during the struggle to prevent the escape. The annual report of the Prison Department says :

> During the rioting which followed the escape attempt and lasted intermittently through the night, several officers received minor injuries requiring first aid, but happily there were no serious injuries suffered by either staff or prisoners. Considerable damage was, however, done by prisoners to furniture and fittings, and to the structure itself, by means of violent physical attacks and arson.

The troubles were only a foretaste of what was to come at Hull, another dispersal prison, in 1976, when three-quarters of a million pounds' worth of damage by rioting prisoners was followed by the court appearance of prison officers, who had allegedly ill-treated them afterwards. The four-day riot at the 109-year-old prison was of 'unprecedented ferocity', according to Mr Gordon Fowler, Chief Inspector of the Prison Service. It put Hull out of action as a dispersal prison for almost a year. In sharp contrast with its former secrecy over Parkhurst, the Home Office, in the face of the devastation and public concern, decided that Mr Fowler's report should be published.

Its findings were in keeping with some of the trends noted earlier in this book, including the difficulty of containing increased numbers of dangerous people. One of Mr Fowler's 'most significant' conclusions was: 'Hull contained an abnormally high proportion of potentially violent prisoners and prisoners with known records of violence, indeed some who had participated in previous disturbances or of acts of disaffection.' Another reason mentioned by Mr Fowler was the effect of the crisis on prison officers: 'The prisoners' daily regime had been curtailed for various reasons, not least staff availability and the budgetary control of prison officers' overtime.'

Mr Fowler stopped short of suggesting that the concept of the dispersal system should be reviewed, but he did recommend that the way the policy was administered should be. He gently added his voice, by implication, to concern at the way policy was shaped without taking properly into account the views of experienced prison officers and governors. He said: 'I would hope that the professional would be allowed to take his rightful place in any deliberations concerning these issues.' In the past, he added, 'those bodies which have grappled with the abstractions of penal policy have advanced sound proposals for dealing with prisoners in the dispersal setting. It may be that their aspirations on occasions have been set a trifle high.'

It is evident from Mr Fowler's report that some confusion existed in the minds of staff about what their role should be in a dispersal prison – not surprisingly, in view of the, to them, bewildering variety of arguments and concepts flowing with the best of intentions from academic institutions, and reflected in some of the non-professional influences on the advisory council about the aims of penal policy and how they should be achieved. To say that is not to be anti-academic but to point out a failure to appreciate sufficiently the day-to-day tension of prison life for the ordinary officer with some practical experience, but sometimes too little training, who has to put those concepts into effect while working in some danger and under enormous pressure.

In Mr Fowler's view the staff at Hull had shown considerable tolerance in the past towards demonstrations and acts of 'concerted indiscipline'. They had 'become conditioned perhaps to an acceptance that this was in accord with current policy. . . . The paradox, of course, is that in a prison where tolerance had been shown, the opportunity for riotous behaviour was that much greater.' In other words, a firmer stance might have prevented trouble.

A vivid picture, essential to the understanding of much that was later to stir the Labour Government into setting up the May Inquiry, is given of how the riot began and developed, after a group of prisoners rushed into A wing, climbed the stairs and took over the landings.

The duty governor, who had also entered the wing, was greeted with a shout of 'you lying bastard' and a fire bucket thrown from an upper landing. The prisoners began to break up furniture and fittings. In B wing others barricaded themselves in the dining-hall. At 20.36 hours, a fire was reported on A wing roof, where prisoners were rampaging.

They had begun to light rags and mattresses and were throwing them on to nearby fuel tanks. Three minutes later a fire was reported on the segregation unit roof. Prisoners dominating the roofs began throwing missiles at the main gate area. By 21.47 hours, there was pandemonium in the prison. At 22.23 hours, the gymnasium was reported to be on fire. At 22.54 hours, prisoners in C wing began to smash up their furniture and fittings and fires were being lit in the wing. Staff were being bombarded by missiles from men on roofs and at 23.06 hours the emergency control room was informed that a man was trying to dig himself out of a cell in C wing.

As attempts were made by staff to regain control of the prison a group of them on an abortive foray into D wing were trapped in various cells, in the library and in the canteen, which had been wrecked and looted. Prisoners in A wing were attempting to break through the walls, which would have allowed them access to D wing and the centre, thereby cutting off the trapped staff.

One officer said:

I saw a senior officer was injured and endeavoured to get him into a corner by the library to avoid the missiles. There were ten of us there. It was pointless trying to stay there because we would all have got injured so we made a dash for the library. We stayed there for about half an hour and them some of us decided to get to the administrative end of D wing – on the third landing. Six of us made a dash and got to the wing annexe. Whilst making the dash I was hit on the left thigh by a slate which made a deep cut. I looked up before the slate struck me and saw a prisoner on the roof – I presume he threw this particular slate. We were some time in the annexe, a principal officer, myself, three detached duty officers and later a senior officer came running round into the annexe.

We were trapped there for over an hour and it was impossible to get into the administration block because of the weight of missiles coming down. By this time, the prisoners were edging off large coping stones. I recognised a prisoner who was shouting, 'Get him in the striped jersey; that's the bastard.' (I was wearing a rugby jersey).

Eventually there was a lull, so I decided to make a dash to the administration block. I was half-way down the stairs when some prisoners who were hidden behind a canopy started to hurl missiles at me. I was protecting my head with the door of a locker. I managed to reach the administration block without further injury.

The initial fuse for the trouble may have been a prisoner's allegations of an assault on him in the segregation unit. The Deputy Governor concluded on the basis of evidence from, among others, the Medical Officer, 'that the allegations were unfounded', the report said. Mr Fowler says the real trigger to devastation was when prisoners gained access to an office and read personal files.

Before the riot, over thirty prisoners demanded to see the prisoner in the segregation unit. A placard displayed on the unit's roof during the riot read 'Stop screws brutality', though some prisoners later said they were referring to what could happen in the future. Mr Fowler's view was: 'It is possible that the incident, certainly on this occasion, might have been avoided.' A request for the Chairman of the Board of Visitors or his deputy to visit would not have thrown doubt upon the propriety of the administration.

In the light of the subsequent court appearances of prison officers, it might seem odd at first sight that after initial allegations of trouble in the segregation unit, little evidence had emerged in the report to indicate that there was any great physical contact between officers and prisoners, though plenty of missiles were thrown. While Mr Fowler mentions in his report 'some preoccupation' by prisoners 'with matters touching on the post-riot situation', he does not go into them.

But he does say: 'There was ... one incident concerning property where, I have reason to believe, certain members of staff may have fallen below the high standards required of the Prison Service, in that when an instruction was given to strip the cells in B wing to make room for surrendering prisoners, this task was carried out with unnecessary zeal and with damage to and disappearance of prisoners' property.'

Mr Fowler's report contained no examination of the disturbing allegations made, by prisoners and campaigners on their behalf, of staff brutality at the end of the riot. The reason was that the Home Office did not ask Mr Fowler to look into them. The task he was given lay specifically between two dates – 31 August and 3 September. So what happened on 4 September could not be his concern. Yet that was the day when, prisoners subsequently told the court, brutality occurred.

George Brock in *The Observer* (8 April 1979) said that the Home Office declined to answer detailed questions about why five months elapsed between the assaults after the riot and the start of the police probe the following February. 'But the picture that emerges throws doubt on whether its internal inquiries could possibly have matched up to the massive inquiry necessary to discover the truth.'

On 4 April 1979 eight of twelve Hull prison staff were found guilty of conspiring to assault inmates.* The remaining four and a thirteenth defendant, a former assistant governor at the prison, had been acquitted. The assistant governor had denied neglecting his duty by failing to prevent, or report, the assaults that occurred, and had moved from Hull to be a prisons administrator.

---

*The eight found guilty were given suspended prison sentences and at the time of writing were appealing against both conviction and sentence.

The question is why five months elapsed between assaults after the riot and the police probe the following February. According to *The Observer*, the police inquiry began after a misspelt letter of a few lines reached the Chief Constable of Humberside Police in January 1977. It had been through normal jail censorship from Winchester Prison and came from a prisoner serving twenty years. It complained simply of 'assaults upon my person'. A team of detectives assembled by the beginning of February were then handed fifteen more complaints made by prisoners and held by the Home Office. Though it is undoubtedly true that the Home Office receives annually a large number of complaints, it ought to have been obvious to any far-sighted administrator that not to give immediate priority to the investigation of the allegations at Hull would give a valuable propaganda advantage to the IRA. Moreover, it would demonstrate that the Home Office was incapable of keeping its own house in order – another argument for reforming the administration of the Prison Service.

When Detective Superintenant Ronald Sagar, Deputy Commander of Humberside CID, began his inquiries, he found that the internal atmosphere among the prisoners gave rise to the usual wall of silence. He was later reported as saying: 'Never before had I been so abused, insulted, aggravated or threatened.'

One of the most important breakthroughs came via an IRA man, who stayed silent while Mr Sagar spent three hours trying to persuade him to speak. The result of Mr Sagar's eventual success was a coded message from the prisoner to his IRA colleagues. The cross-checking of the stories that began to flow in involved interviews with 150 of some of the most unsavoury characters in British prisons – including rapists, murderers and IRA bombers.

However, the witnesses also included a prison officer, by then transferred to Wakefield Prison on compassionate grounds at his own request. He was reported as telling York Crown Court: 'I was sickened at the treatment some prisoners received, although I believe other inmates deserved it.'

The officer said that one prisoner, 'a pathetic homosexual', was knocked to the floor and kicked repeatedly. Another man 'took quite a beating' and was whimpering and crying. An IRA bomber was held by the face and ordered to say 'God save the Queen'.

He agreed under cross-examination that prisoners had turned billiard cues into spears by tying chisels and scissors to them. Inmates also hurled masonry at officers. Some IRA prisoners were in the forefront of the riot.

Before passing sentence on the men, Mr Justice Boreham said that one good thing to emerge from the trial was that never should any group of people, however depraved their conduct, be deprived of the full protection of the law. He accepted that there had been a good deal of exaggeration in evidence presented in court against the prison officers. He also accepted that the injuries caused to the inmates were comparatively slight. Nevertheless, he was in no doubt that prisoners were seriously beaten and kicked.

Though the Fowler report had stopped short of a full examination of the aftermath of the riot and was to that extent constricted, it was a step towards more open examination of what is wrong with the prisons. The greater openness with prisoners and press when trouble flared again at Gartree in 1978 helped to damp down the already serious build-up of disorder, though 150 prisoners had to be transferred to other prisons because of extensive damage to furnishings, fixtures and essential services.

The reason for the disorder at Gartree was concern about the issue of the use of drugs. Prisoners reacted over medical treatment given to a man serving a sentence for murder. The Prison Department's account of events is that he was taken to the prison hospital in a very disturbed condition after an apparent suicide attempt in his cell.

Mr Robert Booth, Deputy Regional Prisons Director for the East Midlands, said there was no truth in allegations that the prisoner was treated without his consent with large doses of tranquillisers not medically necessary and designed to make him passive. According to the 1978 annual report of the Prison Department, the inmates rejected an offer to send two of them to see him in the prison hospital. To try to satisfy fellow inmates that he had not been drugged into passivity or ill-treated, a medical officer allowed him to return to his wing, according to officials at the prison. But the disturbances continued and spread into one of the other wings.

The Medical Committee against Abuse of Prisoners by Drugging replied to Mr Booth by demanding that convicted prisoners should be allowed to call in independent outside psychiatrists for an opinion. Dr Marie O'Shea, consultant psychiatrist in the Connolly Hospital, Birmingham, said that suggestions of a suicide attempt did not fit in with what she had been told by the prisoner's solicitor, who had seen him two weeks earlier 'full of the joys of spring'.

The controversy represents another strand in the argument about medical treatment in prison. According to the Gartree branch of the Prison Officers' Association, seventy-five of the inmates there were mentally ill, and twenty of them so much so that they should have been in special hospitals at Rampton or Broadmoor.

The annual report for 1978 said that, as in the previous two years, the national number of incidents of concerted indiscipline by groups of prisoners averaged thirty. They were spread across the whole prison service and in two cases over 100 prisoners took part. Allegations included complaints against the treatment of individual prisoners, association and visiting arrangements and other aspects of the regime.

To examine the cause and nature of the disturbances, it is necessary to see them in a wider historical context, and to understand the response of prison officers and governors to the worsening crisis in the prison system.

Chapter 9
Prison Officers protest

Prison governors gave their unprecedented warning to Mr Merlyn Rees, the Home Secretary, in October 1978: 'Total breakdown is imminent in the prison system.' The warning was triggered by prison officers' action over a pay claim, but behind their militancy lay a deep frustration. For years they had been forced to contain the worst effects of the growing pressures in the system. Yet their own difficulties had gone largely unrecognised. The emphasis publicly was being put on prisoners' rights and conditions. The fact is that many officers during the course of a career spend more time in total in 'penal slums' than their prisoners.

The words 'penal slums' were used on 17 April 1979 by the Institution of Professional Civil Servants, whose members include 1,400 Home Office staff. They told the May Inquiry in evidence that public health inspectors would use compulsory powers to close many jails if they had jurisdiction.

Two days later public health inspectors demanded access to the prisons. The Environmental Health Officers' Association complained that prisons had 'Crown immunity from local authority inspections'. As a result, health officers were unable to take the necessary steps to protect inmates. Blandly contradicting what many of its own staff in the IPCS evidently felt, the Home Office said that environmental health was the responsibility of prison medical officers and 'we see no reason to suppose they do not do an efficient job'.

Prison officers have complained of poor working conditions for many years, but were prepared to soldier on, in spite of the low esteem in which they felt some people held them. But the cost in terms of stress and family breakdown was seldom mentioned. Nor was it often mentioned that prisoners had a choice as well – the choice of keeping out of prison by not breaking the law.

As anger mounted at a meeting of dissident prison officers from thirty prison establishments on 10 October 1978, Mr Clifford Wilde, of Ford Open Prison, said: 'Society puts away misfits. In doing so it recruits members of the prison service it also regards as misfits. It does not give us the status and certainly not the money we deserve.'

Years of genuine complaints about sinking morale made at annual conferences of the Prison Officers' Association had been discounted by the Government.

As long ago as 1972, Mr Stanley Hodson, an officer at Feltham Borstal, provided a vivid description of the strain officers were under and the failure to heed its effects on them. At Feltham, he said, there were 64 discipline staff to handle 326 youths and men aged between fifteen and twenty-one. All inmates were diagnosed as having personality disorders, Mr Hodson said. They included drug addicts, schizophrenics, sex offenders, violent offenders and those who were simply inadequate.

Eight officers had been off duty for a total of 150 days in four months from injuries received in dealing with violence at Feltham. One officer with twenty years' service had been told by his doctor that he was on the verge of a nervous breakdown and had to have seven weeks off. In four months, four officers had resigned because the job gave them no satisfaction.

Mr Hodson told the conference that staff were being affected by having to cope with violent young offenders who were placed by the Prison Department in overcrowded buildings completely unsuitable to their needs. The staffing arrangements meant that three officers had to cope with sixty highly disturbed boys.

Take away any form of internal discipline, he said, allow them to do as they please, let them grow beards and moustaches and shoulder-length hair, allow them to have pornographic magazines, 'and you have created the first official hippies' borstal. The people who recommend this routine do not have to run the institution, nor do they care or think about the staff who are forced to carry out their policy.'

Officers resigned because they could take no more, he said;

marriages collapsed because officers who tried to cope under stress and strain from long hours of duty changed from young, smiling, enthusiastic men to tired worn-out shells of what they had been, full of frustration. In desperation, they sought to transfer to save themselves from breaking down.

Mr Hodson said: 'The advice of a collective body of men who have spent a great number of years in the Borstal service has been constantly ignored. We have approached our own executive, who have also done their best to help, and still the department ignores the warning.'

Next year, in 1973, it was the turn of Mr Sidney Powell, the Association's National Chairman, to point out the symptoms of the worsening crisis. He described the 1972 demonstrations as 'the most serious challenge to established control, good order and security that the service has had to endure'. He added: 'People in high places refused to accept that the prison service was facing a crisis.' The conference, looking forward ominously but accurately, passed a resolution calling for instruction in riot containment – instruction that had still not been given to many of the officers four years later when the service had to face its worst ever violence.*

Meanwhile, Ashford Remand Centre in Middlesex became the centre of increasingly militant action which was to spread widely in the service. Officers there decided that the prisoners should have no evening classes or association. They staged a token stoppage of an hour when a Crown Court decided not to proceed with a charge against a prisoner of assaulting a prison officer at Ashford. Officers believed their safety was endangered as a result.

Mr John Gunning, of Ashford branch of the POA, whose name was to figure increasingly as militancy in the service mounted, said: 'We work excessive overtime. Staff on their own volition come back in the evening to supervise these services. We think we are running an unnecessary risk.'

Thus did the conference display the growing militancy and growing concern of its members about prison conditions. That militancy was soon to be translated into protest action on a scale which shocked the government. Staff felt under stress and many

---

*Trouble in Wormwood Scrubs in 1979 raised the question as to whether prison officers were being given the most appropriate training for the handling of riots and whether the right tactics were being applied at the right time.

were angry that much publicity appeared to support the prisoners and undervalue the work and worth of staff. In 1972, the anxiety led the POA to threaten a national strike unless manning levels at Gartree Prison, which was to be the scene of much future trouble, were increased. Later in 1972, as a protest against long working hours, the POA instructed all its members not to work during September any more overtime than they were required to do under the terms of a national agreement. The norm was 14 hours a week, but because tasks had steadily increased many staff worked consistently much longer than that. Their action hit courts and disrupted prison life.

Mr Robert Carr, then Home Secretary, promised the annual conference: 'It is my job to provide the tools you need to work successfully and safely. That is why I place such emphasis on a large prison-building programme.'

It was not to be. By 1976 staff and prisoners were faced with a double squeeze caused by increased numbers of inmates and a disastrous cut in capital expenditure as the Labour Government grappled with an economic crisis. In 1976, shocked prison staff heard that by 1979–80 work would begin on only about 800 places for prisoners in new schemes, instead of nearly 5,000 envisaged in the previous White Paper on expenditure in January 1975.* In 1973, when Mr Carr was speaking, about 12,000 prisoners were sharing two or three to a cell built for one. By the end of 1976, the figure was more than 16,000. The planned net growth in the number of prison officers was to be reduced from 3,400 to 3,095 over a four-year period, with none at all in 1979–80. Meanwhile reformers were pointing out that overcrowding could and should be tackled by reducing the prison population rather than by expanding prisons. That could have been done, they claimed, by a much smaller increase in the Probation Service than the proposed

---

*Whereas the intention in 1973 had been to provide 41,000 places in 1976–7, that figure, according to plans published in January 1979, was not to be reached until 1982–3. The forecast expenditure over the period from 1978–9 to 1982–3 assumed that the prison population would increase from an average of 41,970 in 1978–9 to 44,510 by 1982–3, and that building schemes already in progress would provide a net addition of 3,207 places by the end of 1982–3. Starts would be made on one new prison in 1981–2 and two more in 1982–3, according to plans quoted in the May Report.

addition to prison staff; but the Labour Government restrained extra recruitment of probation officers as well.

The Prison Officers were made even angrier by an enforced reduction in overtime, which not only made for greater difficulties in covering duties but reduced take-home pay. As often happens when morale is low, money replaces job satisfaction. The overtime introduced because of staff shortage had given a standard of living people were loath to lose, incidentally stressing the value given officially to long hours of work at the expense of rewards for experience and merit.

The result of the cut-back was industrial action, which included disruptions to court work, restrictions on prisoners' exercise, association, and the operations of prison workshops.

The governors later told the Expenditure Committee of the House of Commons:

> For too long, the Home Office has failed to realise how short of staff prisons were. For years, the service depended on an excessive amount of overtime to make good staff shortages. Staff came to depend on overtime, hence the violent reaction when overtime was reduced by budgetary control (the effect of government cuts). Governors welcome control of overtime: our objection to the introduction of budgetary control was the immediacy and size of the cut and the fact that many desirable developments in treatment and training had to be abandoned as the reduced staff resources were committed to basic tasks. Even in training establishments there has been a reduction in quality of life particularly through the withdrawal of much staff involvement with prisoners.

That withdrawal of involvement meant that staff were less able to sense changes of mood. Hull was one of the places where the effects were most dangerously felt. Mr Fowler's official report on the riot had said that availability of staff and restrictions on prison officers' overtime had curtailed the prisoners' daily routine.

Mr Fowler's strong ideals about the service showed through his factual objectivity when he wrote in his report about the deterioration of the service. The passage is worth quoting in full, because it has general application throughout the service and I know, from conversations over years with many officers, that it accurately reflects how they feel:

> Uncertainty and confusion now exists in the minds of staff at all levels. They see the penalties of involvement with prisoners, the danger of being taken hostage by men who have nothing to lose. They are uncertain about even the use of minimum force – in control terms – and about the extent of their support by higher management. I am not referring here to the use of undue or unauthorised force by staff on individual prisoners, but to the proper control of recalcitrant and violent prisoners – some of whom seek to control the prisoner community by fear.
>
> It may be necessary to go back before we go forward, and rather like the bobby on the beat, ensure real continuity by having regular landing and wing officers.
>
> One of the great truths about running a prison 24 hours a day, every day of the year, however, still remains in 1977. Real security and control, irrespective of the physical devices, lies, insofar as is possible, in knowing what a person is going to do before he does it. This implies *involvement* by staff at all levels and an understanding by the public that support is needed in what is, after all, a demanding and exacting job.

What is particularly shocking about the Hull riot is that ample warning *was* given to the Home Office of impending trouble. Six months before the riot, Mr Kenneth Daniel, General Secretary of the POA, warned of the dangers of overtime restrictions in prisons like Hull. 'We were studiously ignored,' he said. Not only that, but Hull contained an abnormally high proportion of potentially violent prisoners and men with known records of violence. Some had taken part in previous disturbances or in acts of disaffection in dispersal prisons. More than a week before the riot, the Hull Board of Visitors told the Home Office that the jail was 'a powder keg' because of restrictions on prison officers' overtime.

Not only was there a failure in the Home Office to respond to the warnings, but a wider battle had been fought and lost in secret within the Cabinet. Publicly, Mr Roy Jenkins, then Home Secretary, had stated that it would be intolerable if the population reached 42,000 and drastic relief action would be inescapable.

It was a forlorn attempt to impress the rest of the Government with the urgency of the need. In October 1976, that figure was reached. There was no drastic action, because Mr Jenkins had lost political clout and the Cabinet remained unimpressed. He had already in December 1975 used up some room for manoeuvre by agreeing new guide-lines with the Parole Board that more prisoners would be paroled. Thus he kept a promise he had made in August that year that parole should be granted earlier to the kind of prisoners who already received it and to more of the three-fifths who were eligible but did not receive it.

A sharp rise in the number paroled followed. Sir Louis Petch, then the Board's Chairman, told me that the average number of people on parole at any one time in 1976 was 2,750, compared with 1,500 the previous year. The 1976 figure had been equivalent to the population of six fairly large prisons. Nevertheless, the pressure on prisons has continued and the average daily population in 1978 reached 41,796, the highest till then recorded. In March 1980 over 44,800 were crammed into prison.

What was needed and what Mr Jenkins was after when in office was a still greater reduction of pressure. The Jenkins secret plan would have cut the prison population dramatically. In the Autumn of 1975 he took to the relevant Cabinet committee a radical proposal to increase the rate of remission for all prison sentences up to two years from one third to one half. The idea was not accepted.

Evidence for the Cabinet's failure to act comes from Mr Roger Darlington, who had moved to the Home Office as political adviser to Mr Merlyn Rees, Mr Jenkins's successor. In a letter to *The Times* on 7 November 1978, Mr Darlington disclosed:

> I immediately and repeatedly recommended the then and present Home Secretary, Mr Merlyn Rees, to resurrect and implement the proposal. We reached the point of drafting a Cabinet Committee paper, but in the end, the Home Secretary chose not to put the case to his colleagues.
>
> Such an increase in the rate of remission would reduce the prison population immediately and temporarily by up to 4,500 and then eventually and permanently by approaching 4,000.
>
> It would take about three months to plan and six weeks to implement. It would require virtually no expenditure and might

conceivably release some resources. It would need no primary legislation, but simply a statutory instrument to amend the Prison, Detention Centre and Local Review Committee rules.

Others felt, however, that the respite would be only temporary: judges, they believed, would increase sentences so as to return actual time served to its former level, as they are widely assumed to have done in the case of parole, in spite of official denials.

Within prisons, the frustration was increasing. The anger of the local branches of the POA was reflected in a change of policy by the national executive which was to hand greater power to the staff on the spot to act against local grievances. The new policy was that 'forms of action to be pursued on local issues (including sympathetic actions) are matters within the discretion of the local branches concerned'. More recent POA policy has been to allow branches to take protest action on local matters and on the local application of national matters subject to the right of the national executive committee to deplore, fail to endorse, or refuse recognition of such action. It remains declared POA policy not to take industrial action which would directly or indirectly affect the work of the courts – policy that has not always been heeded by angry local branches.

The local POA members quickly took advantage of their new opportunities, as the figures show. Increasing protest action contrasts with the period 1973–5 when it was taken on only twenty-one occasions affecting 15 of the 118 establishments in the system. The following years saw a rapid rise in discontent:

Year	*No. of times branches took action*	*No. of branches involved*
1975	19	13
1976	34	23
1977	42	21
1978	119	63

As fears of severe trouble in Britain's jails grew, the governors decided to speak out more strongly through their union, the Society of Civil and Public Servants, about mistakes in the carrying out of penal policy, some of the worst of which might have been avoided had practical advice been heeded. They had already wanted Mr Jenkins, then the Home Secretary, to think again about his refusal to appoint a serving governor to the Advisory Council on the Penal System so as give it the benefit of more day-to-day practical prison experience. Then, in evidence to the inquiry into the Hull riot, the governors criticised the policy of dispersing high-risk prisoners. A mixture of concentration and better arranged dispersal was suggested by the governors as a possible solution.

By 1977, the mood of the officers had hardened. They accused the Home Office of playing political chess with them and of using the Official Secrets Act to suppress their grievances, which the Home Office denied. Mr F. W. Money, the Association's Chairman, said it had decided to co-operate no longer with budgetary control introduced as part of the Prison Service's contribution to cuts in public spending. He said that a cut of £2 million in man-hours was dangerous, and the Hull riot had borne out their fears.

Action being taken by the prison officers reflected growing impatience, with more emphasis on claims for increased allowances and improvements in quarters and conditions of service. The fall in morale within the service and the general rise in militancy coincided with some criticism of the Association's executive, who had become caught between the Prison Department and increasingly frustrated staff. The national executive committee was censured at the 1978 annual conference for its handling of the Association's financial affairs. The former treasurer had been jailed in September 1977 on pleading guilty to stealing more than £45,000 from the Association's funds. Mr Money said that no other member of the executive or full-time officer was implicated. Delegates rejected a move to remove Mr Daniel, the general secretary, from his post. The vote was followed by a standing ovation for him. The motion to oust him had come from Leicester, Brixton, Cardiff, Rampton and Wandsworth, coincidentally among places where pressures on the system were greatest. Friction between some of the membership and the executive was to worsen, as dissidents voted for yet stronger action.

Part of the disenchantment came over a long-running dispute involving a pay claim for officers at Parkhurst. The officers decided to allow no transfers of prisoners to other prisons or Broadmoor Special Hospital and elsewhere. None were received into Parkhurst either. Court appearances by prisoners were allowed, provided escorts were by Parkhurst officers. There was a ban on visits by lawyers, police, outside probation officers and officials from High Commissions and Embassies to see citizens of their countries detained there. All workshops were closed, including the laundry, which also supplied Camp Hill and Albany Prisons. Civilian instructors were shut out.

The dispute, which originally involved action by Albany and Camp Hill, arose from a campaign for three free ferry passes a year and a claim for cost of living allowance on the grounds that prices are higher on the island than on the mainland. At the height of the conflict five dispersal prisons refused to accept any of the most escape-prone and dangerous prisoners. Onley, in Warwickshire, a young offenders' prison, also stopped receptions for eight weeks. Vehicles were allowed in only for reasons of health, safety or security. No workshops were open there.

Apart from those prisons giving support to Parkhurst officers, nine others were known to have taken some sort of protest action in the previous twelve months over disputes of their own. Not long before, action on such a scale would have been unthinkable, particularly as the course of justice was being interfered with. On 5 April 1978, for example, a young alleged offender, held in custody at Ashford remand centre failed to appear for trial on a purely summary matter. The date of the trial had been fixed since 9 November. Both prosecution and defence were at the court ready to proceed.

The work of other courts was to be disrupted as a result of a dangerous bitterness growing in some of Britain's jails in response to Home Office decisions over back pay. The officers' claim was for retrospective payments for breakfast breaks under a national Civil Service agreement which provided that, in certain circumstances, staff brought on duty earlier than their scheduled starting time could receive 'continuous duty credits' (CDC).

At Ashford, where, as we have seen, trouble had developed on a previous occasion six years before, officers decided to step up their protest. They refused to accept new inmates until someone in authority was prepared to do something about the pressure they were under. Officers there said some cells had been closed because facilities for bathing and obtaining fresh water were inadequate.

Staff who should in theory have had two rest days in seven were being called upon to work, as volunteers, thirteen days out of fourteen. They gave 'staff shortage' as a reason why irate visitors to young people detained at the centre were turned away. Police had to be called, officers said.

Mr Gunning, who at thirty-six years of age had spent fourteen years in the service, told Malcolm Stuart of *The Guardian* in October 1978:

> Experiments with baboons have shown that overcrowding leads to violent reactions. They turn on each other and anyone else that gets in the way – and if you keep three men in an eight by ten cell you get the same reaction.
>
> Here we have been averaging two assaults on staff a week. I'm not just talking about a push in the face but a real thumping that puts a man out of action for a fortnight.

Officers at Ashford had developed a technique of flattening themselves against the corridor wall when they opened a cell door. They said it was a precaution against getting the contents of a full toilet bucket in the face or a battering from a young man caged up for the previous twenty-three hours.

One young man on remand said: 'There's just one bucket for the three of you. They wouldn't allow visits on Saturdays, which was the only time my mum and girl friend could get up. They've closed up all the workshops and in the last five weeks I got just two association periods. Imagine that – in a cell for fifteen days at a time. So you smash up the beds, you thump anyone in sight.'

Ashford was represented at a meeting of officers from about thirty prison establishments which voted on 9 October 1978 to make their protests more widespread. One of the issues was a claim for retrospective payment for lunch and, in some cases, tea breaks. This claim was initially tabled on a national basis but was later pursued by many individual branches with their own variations and threats of industrial action if the claims were not met.

The holding of young people under twenty-one years of age in ill equipped police cells as an alternative to Ashford was a foretaste of trouble to come. Concern grew among prison administrators at the possibility of violence on a massive scale if prisoners seized opportunities opened to them by the officers' actions.

It was that which prompted prison governors, through the Society of Civil and Public Servants, to tell a worried Mr Rees: 'If prison officers totally withdrew their labour for any length of time we will be unable to guarantee either the safe custody of prisoners or the provision of minimum essentials to them.'

The governors added:

> We have yet to experience a serious prisoner reaction to restrictions caused by staff industrial action, but the signs are there. The recent disturbance at Gartree is a salutary reminder of how quickly prisoners can wreck an establishment.
>
> So far we have successfully avoided loss of life during serious disturbances, but if the present trend continues, there will be a serious loss of control, which has to be quelled by armed intervention by another service. In such circumstances there is a possibility of both staff and prisoners being killed. There are precedents in other prison systems.

The governors criticised the Home Office for producing no initiative and saw 'no sign of firm leadership in this crisis'.

In Scotland, officers voted on 15 November to begin a work-to-rule selective strike action, to shut down prisons for four-hour periods, and to ban overtime. The officers wanted a segregation unit at Porterfield Prison – known among prisoners as 'the cage' – to be made available for use. The unit was the centre of violent clashes between prison officers and inmates in 1972. That led to the opening of a special unit at Barlinnie Prison, Glasgow, which has since become internationally respected as a prison within a prison where the regime can be relaxed. Mr John Reston, Secretary of the Scottish Prison Officers' Association, said that his members in Scotland's twelve prisons were deeply worried by the growing number of attacks on them. Official figures showed that up to November in 1978 sixty officers had been assaulted, compared with fifty-two attacks the previous year.

In Scotland, there had been industrial action in 1972 lasting six weeks at Longriggend remand institution, over alleged delays in the provision of a staff club. In 1973, a work-to-rule in the last half of June at Barlinnie was caused by the allocation of basic staff houses to governor grades. The use of the Inverness unit was discontinued in 1972 in the face of criticism, mainly from outside the service. Ministerial assurances that the unit would be used when occasion required removed the national threat. But unofficial action by staff at eight establishments involved working to rule and a ban on overtime for lengths of time of up to three weeks.

While Mr Rees publicly dismissed as 'much too alarmist' suggestions that things would get out of control, his civil servants had been privately concerned some weeks before at the possibility of a breakdown. The Home Office was in the difficulty of not knowing quite how to deal with the officer's co-ordinating action. As far as the Home Office was concerned, the dissidents were acting independently of the Association's executive, if not unofficially. Officially the Home Office could deal only with the hard-pressed POA headquarters.

The men were not firebrands, but deeply frustrated. Their difficulty was how to take action to draw attention to long-standing grievances without damaging the welfare of prisoners – a dilemma almost impossible to resolve. They pointed out that they had tried every other means of trying to persuade the Home Office and government that urgent action was needed to deal with the crisis in prisons that almost nobody seemed to care about. There are few votes to be won at election time by politicians campaigning for better prisons.

I asked one officer, en route to seek the support of the national executive, how he would judge a good colleague. He replied without hesitation: 'By the way he treats the prisoners.'

They were baffled by the mysteries of the working of the Home Office bureaucracy. They knew there was something called 'Estabs Division III' and that letters came out of it signed by a woman. Was she someone's secretary? one officer wondered.

There was a Director General for the Prison Service, but, like God, his active existence had to be taken on faith. His name was unknown to most officers I met. He certainly was not like them, they felt. The consensus seemed to be that he might be a good civil servant, but what was he doing running the service? Why was it in such a mess? What could be done about it? At least the pay issue was something worth fighting over. They didn't really relish long hours of overtime for its own sake, as it put a strain on them and their families, but the pay might make it worth doing, they said. Indeed, some officers, known to their colleagues as 'overtime bandits', were prepared to work excessively for large sums.

The effect was to distort earnings to such an extent that overtime worked by prison officers amounted, on average, to almost 60 per cent of their basic pay; and average gross earnings were greater than those for assistant governors II and only slightly below those for chief officers II. Though few employees in British industry generally work on average more than sixty hours a week, over a quarter of junior prison officers were doing so. Comparisons between occupations bring out the amount a prison officer, below principal officer, can earn. No fewer than 94·3 per cent of them received overtime pay, compared with 58·5 per cent of workers in all manual occupations. That gave prison officers below principal officer gross weekly average earnings of £129·10, including £47·80 overtime. The comparable figure for non-manual occupations was £113·00 gross, including £3·90 for overtime; and the total gross weekly earnings of those in manual occupations were £93·00, of which £14·00 came from overtime working. (The figures are from the May Report.)

The high prizes made possible by overtime and other payments for working odd hours were made the more tantalising to prison officers by agreements so complicated that different people interpreted them in different ways – a recipe for trouble. They said that it was not until a prison officer had pointed out that the agreement made it possible for the government to pay money for certain meal breaks that it was realised that officers might be owed money for them. As to who might be entitled it, that depended on interpretation (the Howard League for Penal Reform quoted the case of one bemused officer asking a prisoner with financial expertise to work out his entitlement).

What made it all even more confusing was that officers getting the extra money in one prison were told that they were not entitled to it when they were transferred to another prison to do roughly similar work. The suspicion hardened that the Home Office was trying to do them down, or at least was fighting every inch of the way to prevent them getting their due.

But others within the Home Office were convinced that the officers were jumping in with claims in the belief that they had the Government on the run in the pre-election period. According to this view, Mr Rees would not dare to allow real trouble in the prisons for fear of giving Conservatives much-needed votes on the law and order issue.

By now, the dissidents had so little faith in the Home Office that even an announcement by Mr Rees in the House of Commons that there would be an urgent independent inquiry into prisons and the way they were run failed to change their minds about taking action. He told MPs that the inquiry would examine the organisation and management of the prison system in the United Kingdom, including its use of resources and working arrangements, conditions in penal establishments, and the structure, pay and conditions of service.

Such was the gap in understanding between the Home Office and the men in 1978 that they refused to accept any assurance that the inquiry would consider the issue they were worried about until it had actually been given to them in writing. When they got it, they began calling off their action. Mr Rees said on 6 November that 27 of 113 prison service establishments were involved in protest action, not including Parkhurst, where there was an outstanding dispute over a claim for special allowances.

Even Mr Rees was agreeing by 21 November that the breakdown of industrial relations had been the catalyst that had brought the service close to 'real catastrophe'. He admitted to a conference of boards of visitors that the service would be inadequate to support the criminal justice system for some time to come. 'To make it adequate will require massive extra resources,' he said.

Politically one can see why Mr Rees might want to have a plan for action ready for the general election campaign, in which law and order was to be one of the main issues. He called for the report by March. But he and his advisers totally underestimated the immensity of the problems facing the service and therefore the nature of the task he was giving the Inquiry team, under its Chairman, Mr Justice May.

The Inquiry team did not report by March, and in the six months after it was set up industrial action took place on thirty-one occasions at twenty-five different establishments. And that was in addition to the general Civil Service industrial action over pay in April 1979, which affected 105 establishments.

The May Inquiry team did not report until 31 October, by which time there was a new Conservative administration. Immediately, the Report became part of a power struggle that had already been fought out behind closed doors for fifteen years or more – to decide who was to control the prison system, the professionals or the civil servants.

Chapter 10
The Role of Whitehall

The confusion and loss of morale which have helped to bring the Prison Service to the brink of disaster were predicted as long ago as 1963 by opponents of Whitehall's successful attempts, made then and subsequently, to gain greater bureaucratic power over the prison system.

The changes introduced since then have fuelled such strong feelings that prison governors told the May Inquiry in February 1979: 'In the evidence received from our members the universal condemnation of the present organisational structure of the prison service was striking in its anguish and virulence.'

The growth of bureaucracy followed moves by Whitehall mandarins and ministers, introduced with some deviousness against fierce criticism in and out of Parliament. Their purpose was the absorption of the old Prison Commission, set up in 1877 to be responsible for prisons, within the control of the Home Secretary.

The bid to abolish the Commission succeeded only at the third attempt, begun in 1961 with the Criminal Justice Act. Abolition proposals in a 1938 Bill, abandoned on the outbreak of war, were reintroduced in a Bill of a decade later, but were later withdrawn by the Home Secretary in the face of opposition during the committee stage.

The tactics worked out in Whitehall were for Mr Henry Brooke to move in the Commons that 'the Prison Commissioners Dissolution Order 1963, a draft of which was laid before this House on 5 February, be approved'. Constitutionally, he said, 'it is anomalous and misleading that the Commission should appear to be a separate and independent body'.

MPs do not like being taken so much for granted. Referring to 'great interest' in the issue, Miss Alice Bacon, MP for Leeds South, complained that the subject warranted a Bill, 'which we could have discussed properly and which we could have amended'.

That was not Whitehall's idea at all. For Miss Bacon pointed out that the proposal was tucked away as a 'rather incongruous part' of the Criminal Justice Act 1961, which dealt chiefly with the treatment of offenders under twenty-one. Section 23 was to give the Home Secretary power to bring in an Order in Council to absorb the Prison Commissioners within the Home Office. 'Now we have before us an Order which we must either approve or disapprove. We must either take it or leave it.

'It is only because Hon. members on both sides objected that we are having adequate time to debate this proposal. Indeed, in spite of the assurances given by the previous Home Secretary, it was originally suggested that we should start to debate this important matter at about 10 or 11 o'clock at night.'

It has to be remembered that in 1963 the Government had a majority big enough to ensure that what was willed in Whitehall went through. The whips could see to that. Effective power had passed from the floor of the House, which has since caused so much anger among back-bench MPs that there have been partly successful moves to try and strengthen the Select Committee system and other means of scrutinising policymaking and the way it is operated by Whitehall: in other words to curb the power of the Civil Service.

Thus it was not incongruous that, when the issue of the Commissioners' future was earlier discussed in the House of Lords, the Government had a decided majority even though, as Miss Bacon put it, apart from speeches by the Minister of State at the Home Office, and the Lord Chancellor, every speech was against the Order.

So was most informed opinion against the change, according to Miss Bacon, including that of *The Lancet, The Observer, The Economist* and *Sunday Telegraph* and, on several occasions, *The Times*. The Howard League for Penal Reform also opposed the change.

A leading article in *The Times* that very day had said:

It is only to be expected that serious fears should exist as to how far the absorption of the Commission would encourage the growth of a Civil Service mentality, a loss of the old *esprit de corps* and an increasing avoidance of public scrutiny. Rather than this fate the government should be thinking in terms of encouraging both the existing Home Office departments to establish freer direct relations with the world at large. The government have already recognised that substantial misgivings exist on these scores.

The compulsive avoidance of public scrutiny which *The Times* forecast later resulted in annual reports omitting to cover properly, and sometimes not at all, the most pressing matters troubling the service. The loss of *esprit de corps* has led to a bitterness and preoccupation with money in lieu of job satisfaction, though, of course that tendency is not confined to the Prison Service. More opportunity to give information to the world at large is what defensive governors and discontented prison officers have long been calling for.

Though the old Prison Commission was not without its faults (some prison officers thought it autocratic), MPs defending it felt it had the overriding virtue of independence and was a depository of practical experience that won for it in its time a far higher reputation than is now possessed by its more bureaucratic successors.

It is true that there were complaints about prisons then which still have a familiar ring – for example, about overcrowding, though in 1963 the prisons held only 30,000 inmates, compared with the 44,800 in March 1980.

But, as the formidable Mrs E. M. Braddock, MP for Liverpool, Exchange, put it, 'a body slightly outside the Home Office, which was by way of being an adviser to the Home Office, is to be removed and one method of drawing attention to difficulties will be removed from the prisoners'. As for criticism of the Commission, she complained that 'the recommendations and suggestions of the Commissioners have not been accepted by the Home Office'.

In reply, Mr Brooke said that there was not the slightest sign that progress was being held up by the Home Office. He told the House :

'I have heard it suggested that integration threatens a take-over by administrative and executive civil servants of the functions of the trained staff of the prison service. That is completely untrue. The position and the work of the professional prison service, from the Commissioners who have been trained in the prison service, through to the prison officers, will be wholly unaffected by this Order.

In his efforts to get the measure through Parliament, Earl Jellicoe, a Government Minister, had told the House of Lords about the prospects for promotion of professionals in the service. 'It is not impossible in my view to conceive of that imaginary young officer at Wakefield one day becoming head of the Prison Department or, for that matter, Permanent Under-Secretary.'

Only three and a half years after Mr Brooke's and Lord Jellicoe's fine words, Lord Mountbatten was to report of the Prison Service: 'The head office has clearly to some extent lost touch with the establishments under its control.' Though he thought the abolition of the Commissioners and the creation of the Prison Department at the Home Office to be 'necessary in itself', he commented:

> The Prison Commission was thought of as an identifiable body of known Commissioners, with a particularly well-known chairman, whereas the multiplicity of the functions of the Home Office made the Prison Service, or many of its members at least, feel that they had lost their separate identity when their superior officers became merged in so large and so diverse an organisation.

Worried about the increasingly poor morale in the service, Lord Mountbatten said it was essential to appoint a professional head of the service: 'He must be a real commander or leader in every sense of the word. . . . The professional head should also become a figure known to the general public, and not only to that part of it which is seriously interested in prison matters. I regard this as a highly desirable consequence of the removal of anonymity.'

Lord Mountbatten saw such a figure as the top link between the Home Secretary and the service, so that the staff's point of view could be heard. (Much of the protest action in recent years has been because staff have felt that their views have been unheard.) Lord Mountbatten went on to say about the proposed head of the service:

> His duties should go far beyond inspection and involve command and leadership functions as well as responsibility for advising the Home Secretary on all professional matters.

The first man to be given this task was Brigadier Mark Maunsell, a director of Gallaher Ltd who had been Chief of Staff in several top army jobs. He began work in 1967 with the title of Inspector General.

One of Earl Mountbatten's assessors for the inquiry was Sir Robert Mark, then plain Mr Mark, Chief Constable of Leicester, who later, as the Metropolitan Police Commissioner, did for the police what the Mountbatten report clearly had in mind for the Inspector General of the Prison Service.

> I am convinced that an outstanding man must be found as the first holder of this new post, since he must create it and endow it with the prestige it needs. The Prison Service must soon get to know him personally and appreciate his qualities. They must have confidence that he has quickly obtained such a grip on their problems that he can be relied upon to present their views to the Home Secretary.

Brigadier Maunsell was appointed by Mr Roy Jenkins, then Home Secretary. They had years before become friends while working together for the John Lewis Partnership, where Mr Jenkins was economic adviser. Lord Mountbatten's private view at one stage was that the job should go to a retiring Chief of the Imperial General Staff, but he also knew and trusted Brigadier Maunsell through war service. The Brigadier had served under Lord Mountbatten as 'representative of the Supreme Allied Commander' in what reverted to be French Indo-China and as Commander of the Control Commission there. He left the Army in 1955 and went to Gallaher Ltd, from which he was seconded.

What happened to Brigadier Maunsell was explained by the Prison Officers' Association in its evidence to the May Inquiry:

Brigadier Maunsell was a popular figure in the prison service throughout his tenure in office. However, the Civil Service is not prone to accepting individualism and it became clear at a relatively early stage that the Inspector General was being reduced to a titular rather than realistic head of the Prison Service. . . . Many of the problems now being faced are attributable to the very bureaucracy which effectively neutralised the status of the Inspector General.

The POA, calling for organisational changes and more independence for the service, told the May Inquiry:

On balance the Association favours a recognised and identifiable head of the service. It welcomed the appointment of the Inspector General more that a decade ago and was saddened to see his role and function eroded in a manner which culminated with his departure. The Association considers that the head of the service should be responsible and accountable for the pay and conditions of his staff. He should personally involve himself in commenting to the news media when prison matters attract public interest and he should have a direct and ready access to the Home Secretary.

Whereas Lord Mountbatten had clearly had in mind someone to lead the prison service, his views, as shown by subsequent events, seem not to have prevailed, to the dismay of many in the Prison Service.

The weakness of Lord Mountbatten's recommendations about the post of Inspector General was that they did not specify precisely how the internal bureaucracy of the Home Office could accommodate a charismatic leader. That ambiguity was to enable the Civil Service eventually to consolidate its control over the Prison Service. Almost as soon as Brigadier Maunsell took over his job, he sought to discover what his terms of reference were and what authority he had to carry them out. The weakness of his position quickly became clear to those in touch with him.

There was already a senior civil servant chairing a Prisons Board within the Home Office and another civil servant of slightly lesser rank who was known as Head of the Prison Department. But the

Brigadier had direct contact with his old friend, Mr Jenkins, at ministerial level, and outside the Home Office he made friends with the Prison Officers' Association. As long as he could meet the Home Secretary informally, he could remain an additional and direct link between the minister and the rank and file. Brigadier Maunsell's tours of prisons brought him into close contact with men and governors. Trust grew from frankness on both sides – a trust which has many long-serving members of the POA looking back nostalgically.

It is ironical that some of the weaknesses which the Brigadier found over ten years ago and pointed out were among those which have since been the cause of so much discontent: personnel management and prison officers' quarters, notably the quarters of officers suffering the dampness of Dartmoor, are two issues that spring to mind.

Once Mr Jenkins left to become Chancellor of the Exchequer and was replaced by Mr Callaghan, the link between staff and Minister could hardly be quite the same. Brigadier Maunsell's idea that an organisation and methods team (a Home Office team, at that) should be brought in to suggest improvements in the Prison Department's administration was in fact a recognition of where the power lay.

Brigadier Maunsell's original two years' secondment from Gallaher Ltd was due to end in 1969. Mr Callaghan nevertheless asked him to stay on for a further two years. But four or five months before the end of that second period Brigadier Maunsell left the Prison Department. Had he received the authority Mountbatten had wanted for him, the story might have had a different ending.

One clue to what happened is the organisational chart (so beloved of bureaucracies) that always looks at first sight like the family tree of one of the more fecund feudal dynasties. Sprouting beneath the Director General of the Prison Service (a civil servant) in the 1969 annual report was a fine bureaucratic foliage from the twigs of four main branches – three controllers (of planning and development; administration; and operations) and one director of the prison medical service.

But where was Brigadier Maunsell's post on the chart? No twigs for him. His position on the tree had no foliage. As the anonymous report of the Prison Department for 1969 said: 'Except as a member of the Prisons Board, he has no executive responsibility.' But he was responsible for inspecting and reporting on the efficiency of regions and establishments – in other words he was to be an inspector, but no general.

As Brigadier Maunsell, like any good old soldier, faded away (he left in 1970), the bizarre consequences of the bureaucracy created began to cause frustrations in the service. It emerged that the Director General and Prison Department had no executive authority over any of its staff. They could offer advice, but that was all. Real power lay elsewhere, with something called Establishments Division III, which does not come under the Director, but which has been the subject of much swearing over pints of beer in prison officers' clubs up and down the land.

Most often officers could be heard saying that they wanted 'someone like Sir Robert Mark to speak up for them'. 'There is no leadership,' they complained. 'Who will answer prisoners' lies about us?' they lamented.

The sense of clear direction that a disciplined service needs had gone. Symptomatic of the staff's attitude was the strength of feeling about the decline in status of the chief officer, the equivalent of a sergeant-major in the Army, and a figure of discipline. One of the leaders of the militants behind the action which led to the Inquiry spoke with real bitterness to me at the annual conference of the POA about the way 'my Chief at my prison' had been treated during a visit by the May Inquiry team: 'Do you know what he was down on the timetable to do? To serve coffee. That was what he was thought fit for: my Chief, with all his years of experience. If that's how they treat him, what do they think of me?' The 1979 annual conference of the Association passed a resolution demanding extra money for experience gained in long service.

Concerned about the erosion of the chief officer's standing, the POA said in its evidence to Mr Justice May:

> A Chief Officer is the head of the discipline staff. There is no easy way to become a Chief Officer. The most junior members of these grades have the best part of a quarter of a century prison experience behind them at the time of appointment. Prison

officers, regardless of where they serve, invariably see their first loyalty as being towards the Chief Officer. . . . There is an ingrained suspicion that the Home Office wishes to phase Chief Officers out.

Very often a chief officer takes home less pay than men in ranks below him because of the overtime they can earn, yet he is the key to the discipline of the service.

Since the nature of the prison population has become more volatile, sudden switches of mood demand sensitive and flexible responses and depend much upon day-to-day frustrations and the exploitation of them by subversives. In the dispersal prisons, where some of Britain's toughest inmates are to be found, officers with little training can feel particularly vulnerable and their sense of isolation can be dangerous. The self-confidence that a disciplined service can bring is being eroded.

Prison officers have seen numbers of specialists – such as psychologists and welfare officers – brought in, leaving the officers to do mostly the unsatisfying mechanical routines of the day, such as locking, unlocking, maintaining order, escort duties, the mainly negative tasks of watching, waiting, controlling, enforcing. With fewer opportunities for constructive work with prisoners, there are dangerous signs of a withdrawal from contact with them. Weak prisoners are then more easily dominated and intimidated by tough men at the top of their hierarchy.

The governor no longer has sufficient authority to govern as many would wish. The governors have said in evidence to the May Inquiry:

> Governors can find themselves dealing with three or four different parts of headquarters on a relatively minor matter, co-ordinating the various responses, and then involving the regional office. While these lengthy discussions are going on, the establishment may be left completely in the dark. The governor then has the task of defending his superiors, of dealing with the resultant anxiety, frustration or outright aggression of inmates or staff or both, and of trying to restore confidence and repair relationships once the decision has been made.

The Prison Officers' Association agrees:

> Decision taking is a protracted affair and there appears to be a natural inclination to make no decision at all as opposed to the risk of making what could be seen as a wrong decision. This in turn lends itself to hesitancy, delay, confusion and inevitable dispute. Much of the anger arising from the inadequacies of the system are either directed at local governors or at the national officers of the POA.

The feeling among the staff that their status and position are under threat is explained by what they perceived as the attitude of Establishments Division III, which staff said, sought to treat them in the same way as administrative group civil servants, despite the very different working conditions. The governors report: 'In one dispersal prison recently, the entire stability of the regime was placed in jeopardy and considerable personal distress caused as a result of unwillingness to resolve swiftly and sympathetically a problem over catering staff, and this despite representations at Prison Board level.'

The protest which so alarmed the Cabinet and resulted in the setting up of the May Inquiry stemmed from such ineffectiveness. As the POA puts it:

> Many conditions related to the prison officers deal with the unique nature of their employment about which there are no adequate general civil service rules, precedents or practices. The dispute over certain continuous duty credits [part of the reason for the protest action by prison staffs] is an example of this problem. It is also clear that a relatively simple principle – the status of unscheduled meal breaks [another cause of bitterness] – was complicated out of all recognition by the application of civil service rules intended for different circumstances.

What angers governors and prison officers alike is, as governors said in evidence to the Expenditure Committee, that 'against all principles of sound management theory and practice, the organisation which has accountability for the action of its staff has no authority in negotiations; and the organisation that does have negotiating authority has no accountability for the result. Consequently there is an understandable feeling of frustration, recognition of impotence and inevitably overcaution and delay.'

Not only have staff had to cope with a loss of faith by the experts in what prisons are for, not only have they to handle larger numbers of more dangerous prisoners than at any time in their experience, but their pride in some of the better traditions of their job has been undermined by critics, sometimes in official positions, who do not understand their value. The character of the service was also diluted by a necessarily rapid expansion in numbers. Between 1966 and 1968 there was an 88 per cent increase in numbers of prison officers from 8,000 to 15,000.

Like the police they are drawn from a pool which includes the services. The experience of soldiering, in which orders given by persons in recognisable positions of authority were carried out, often because men's lives depended upon it, helped in the past to maintain the discipline of the Prison Service. Rapid expansion of the service has brought into it people with attitudes bred in industry, where authority is questioned more. On top of that, the training they get in the Prison Service is inadequate for the tasks they have to perform. And hours of duty, of course, have often been rewarded at the expense of financial incentives to officers to obtain better qualifications.

Officers have become rebellious. Like feudal barons without a suitable prince to command their loyalty, and with their Association caught in an understandable state of confusion and seeming inadequacy through failure in Whitehall, the officers took action to obtain answers that many of them thought were forthcoming in no other way.

Once the Inquiry was set up and the barriers of secrecy began to be broken down, more causes of frustration began to emerge, this time in evidence published by boards of visitors. The Board at Strangeways Prison, Manchester, accused the Prison Department of being lethargic in its dealings with its own employees' and prisoners' complaints. Some of the militancy in the Prison Officers' Association could be laid at the door of the Home Office, the Board said. Its strongly worded memorandum said that the Home Office must appreciate that it was the prison officers who were at the sharp end of the business. 'It is only sensible, to say nothing of courteous, to give them slightly better attention than has been the case in the past.' The Board suggested that someone with experience of the Prison Service should head the Prison Department with authority and be in a position to give orders and directions.

The Board disclosed that it was an ultimatum by prison officers not to admit any more to the overcrowded young prisoners' wing that produced 'dramatic and lasting effects'.

According to the Board of Visitors at Walton Prison, Liverpool, the Home Office Prison Department was too monolithic and remote. Staff morale at Walton had been low for a long time. 'We relate this to a number of factors, including the remoteness of top managements in the Home Office, the seemingly unnecessarily long delays in obtaining decisions from London, the inadequate consultation machinery, and the narrow and restricted field in which the governor is allowed to operate, especially in relation to industrial matters.' The Board also criticised delays at the Home Office in dealing with prisoners' petitions, which were matters of paramount importance.

The Board of Visitors at Leeds Prison, which was built in the 1840s to hold about 600 prisoners and in 1968 rarely had fewer than 1,100, said that even basic security tasks could not always be done. The Board blamed the Home Office for not acquiring land nearby due for slum clearance to build a remand wing, extend the hospital and improve the quality of life for inmates and staff.

After five prison officers were injured in February 1979 at Walton Prison, Liverpool, and prisoners staged a rooftop protest, the Governor, Mr William Driscoll, allowed in press and television cameras. He said: 'The violence was the result of frustration. The situation the prisoners are in "normally" is appalling. On average they are in their cells for 16 hours a day. We have 285 prisoners three to a cell, 892 two to a cell and 233 single cells in a prison designed for 800.' The violence began as a result of protest action by 460 officers over a meal break allowance. Some prisoners were in their cells for up to 23 hours a day. Mr John Bartell, a prison officers' spokesman, said: 'We had a full-scale riot here only four years ago and since then the only money spent on the place was a new office block for the management. The rest of the place is still a slum.'

One of the reasons for the incompatibility of civil service style administration and the need for quick response by a flexible management within a prison is shown by the POA in evidence to the May Inquiry about what happens when a local dispute threatens and the POA's national chiefs want to smooth things out with the local governor.

First, POA headquarters must contact the Prison Department's Establishments Division, which in turn contacts the controllerate of operations, which contacts the regional office, which contacts the prison governor. The answer comes back via the same route.

As the POA says: 'Lines of communication within the managerial machine lend themselves to delay and indecision and, in turn, encourage the use of local industrial action as the only legitimate means by which positive decisions can be arrived at without undue delay.

'The Association recommends that local management should be given more authority in its dealings with POA.'

And if that can happen to men with a trade union, think what can happen to people without one – the prisoners.

Chapter 11
The May Inquiry

1 TACKLING THE HOME OFFICE

After relations between prison staff and the Home Office had worsened and industrial action disrupted regimes, Mr Merlyn Rees, Home Secretary, announced the membership of the May Committee and its terms of reference. (A list of members of the Committee is given as an appendix on page 160.)

The Inquiry began work in a spirit of optimism, amid hopes that it would not only be able to remove the causes of bitterness among prison staff but would produce a new philosophy and programme for prisons with a vision valid for the twenty-first century. But the choice of names produced some murmurings among prison staff that they did not include anyone – a former governor, for example – who had direct experience of the day-to-day life in prison.

The Home Secretary gave the Committee the following terms of reference:

> To inquire into the state of the prison services in the United Kingdom; and having regard to:
> (a)   the size and nature of the prison population, and the capacity of the prison services to accommodate it;
> (b)   the responsibilities of the prison services for the security, control and treatment of inmates;
> (c)   the need to recruit and retain a sufficient and suitable staff for the prison services;
> (d)   the need to secure the efficient use of manpower and financial resources in the prison services;

to examine and make recommendations upon
- (i) the adequacy, availability, management and use of resources in the prison services;
- (ii) conditions for staff in the prison services and their families;
- (iii) the organisation and management of the prison services;
- (iv) the structure of the prison services, including complementing and grading;
- (v) the remuneration and conditions of service of prison officers, governors and other grades working only in the prison services, including the claim put forward by the Prison Officers' Association for certain "continuous duty credit' payments and the date from which any such payments should be made;
- (vi) allowances and other aspects of the conditions of service of other grades arising from special features of work in the prison services;
- (vii) working arrangements in the prison services; including shift systems and standby and on call requirements;
- (viii) the effectiveness of the industrial relations machinery, including departmental Whitley procedures, within the prison services.

The disappointment and anger which prison staffs at all levels have felt about the May Report can best be understood in the light of earlier events. They help to explain much of the strong feeling about the Civil Service and are an ingredient of unrest in prisons.

Before the May Committee had a chance to put forward proposals to improve the morale of the Prison Service, that morale had been undermined by revolutionary changes proposed in 1974 by a Home Office management review team, about which controversy has rumbled ever since. Since their report was first produced before a POA annual conference three or four years ago it has been constantly discussed by all concerned with the service whenever its future has been debated.

Many in the Prison Service saw the Home Office team's proposals as a means of extending the power of the bureaucracy to prisons themselves. The plans, born when the treatment philosophy reached its zenith, were intended to destroy the old hierarchical command structure of the service, which most serving officers regard as essential to its discipline. In its place was to be a bureaucratic formula called 'management by activity', with the positions of administrative officers (civil servants) upgraded and the governor's strong right hand, the chief officer, removed from his present key position. The team concluded that Chief Officer I posts were redundant and that Chief Officer II posts should be limited to the function of perimeter controllers at busy local prisons.

But the report threw chief officers a bone:

> This does not mean, however, that the officers now occupying these posts are incapable of performing the new functions described; there are many precedents for amalgamating grades so closely parallel in status and pay as the Assistant Governor I and Chief Officer grades, and as the requirements for unit management develop in the long term at all establishments, there may well be a case for amalgamating Assistant Governors II and Principal Officers, thus effectively creating a largely one class service in unit management.

(Sceptics might recall the argument which was used in 1963 by Earl Jellicoe when he dangled before professionals the prospect of promotion to the highest echelons of the Civil Service as a reward for the destruction of the old Prison Commission.)

As if to underline the incompatibility of the Civil Service ethos with the sort of prison service Lord Mountbatten had in mind and Brigadier Maunsell was supposed to personify, the review team say: 'Charismatic "leaders" [the inverted commas are in the text] can no longer rely on other people to provide the solid foundation on which their style of leadership depends; in common with trends in outside life, prison managers must now accept a requirement to work perhaps harder and certainly more systematically and with more foresight than their staff.'

Not only was the service to be more greyly bureaucratic, but greater power was to flow outwards from headquarters. The team say: 'The task at local level is to carry out HQ policies with the most economic and effective expenditure of resources and that local management is not free to add to or to reduce its designated activities according to its own assessment of penal priorities.'

Given the way that the old style of discipline in the service had been undermined, it is not surprising that the review team found 'widespread disagreement amongst managers [note how 'governors' have become translated already in the vocabulary] about their objective roles and an almost universal lack of any identifiable management methods above basic procedure level'. The team added: 'Local managers themselves were unhappy about their positions in that they felt that their guide-lines on briefs were inadequate and that whatever managerial initiative they took, they would almost certainly be open to criticism from one official quarter or another. In our view, such a situation required a radical reappraisal from first principles.'

(Yet the review team had already, by a remarkable process of double-think, stated that far from managers being allowed ample room for initiative 'the task at local level is to carry out HQ policies'. The logic leading to 'a radical reappraisal from first principles' is therefore non-existent.)

Quite unconsciously, of course, the Home Office had fallen into the trap which it well knows is employed by radicals the world over when bent on revolutionary change: first weaken an institution then, when it fails to function properly, use its weakness as a reason for destroying and replacing it. The word used by the Home Office to describe the actions of such people is 'subversion', something of which it can hardly accuse itself.

Nobody is suggesting that civil servants set out with subversion in mind, but the effect of the tentacular growth of bureaucracy, doubtless with the best of intentions, is the same. The irony is that the cries of frustration from members of the service are then treated wrongly as subversive, a classic example of dealing with effects rather than causes.

There is a curious reference in the Home Office management review to creating 'modules', which it defines as 'mutually compatible sub-organisations'. The organisation of an establishment might 'consist of a number of separate modules, selected from a range of modules, each of which could be tailored to achieve a generally recognised policy objective (such as the assessment, treatment and progress of inmates) under a particular set of conditions. Should headquarters then decide to change a particular policy objective or the particular conditions under which it should be applied in an establishment, it would then be merely a question of replacing one or other of the existing organisational modules at that establishment by an appropriate substitute without upsetting the remainder of the organisation.'

The POA said roundly in its evidence to the May Committee on Management Review Stage III:

> In brief, the document looked forward to a prison service of the future, where uniformed prison officers were little more than faceless ciphers providing a background policing function and where specialised employment was undertaken by specialists recruited for that purpose.
>
> The reaction of the Association to MR3 was both marked and predictable. The document, and its blueprint for the future, were unacceptable. The introduction of public expenditure cuts effectively prevented any progress being made on the more contentious parts of the report but the Association would be failing in its duty to the Inquiry if it did not make plain its deep suspicion of the intentions of management regarding the introduction of MR3 and the likely reaction of the Association to any attempt at its introduction.
>
> As mentioned elsewhere in this submission, it is the intention of the Association to broaden the spectrum of employment of prison officers. This is not consistent with acceptance of MR3 which has been rejected as an organisational concept by the Association. In this regard the Association wishes to make it clear beyond any possibility of misunderstanding, that it considers the MR3 'philosophy' an insult to its members' legitimate aspirations.

To the bureaucracy, the merit of a modular scheme is obvious. Changes can take place to suit headquarters with minimal fuss. There would be no possibility of opposition from 'charismatic leaders' – just an imperceptible shading of the bureaucracy into a deeper grey.

By themselves the chief officers – who have plenty of charisma – have little influence on the internal politics that will decide their future, being only a minority of the POA. Yet it is their loyalty to the service, plus the fact that they are the repository of its collected wisdom handed down over the years, that gives them their unique strength if used in the right way.

One example of the way the review team's proposals, applied in detail, would radically change the service and weaken morale is in the following paragraph: 'We suggest that, as in other specialist fields, the future trend in catering must be towards a fully professional service and that the balance of advantage lies in the gradual phasing out of the prison officer class in the catering service and its replacement by suitably qualified civilian officers.' What may seem logical to the outsider is, in fact, naive.

The naivety lies in a failure to comprehend that there is much more to working in the kitchens of a busy prison than serving good meals, important though that is. Staff at Aylesbury Prison, for example, are enthusiastic in teaching young prisoners how to be chefs. They run courses, complete with classroom and blackboard, of a surprising degree of sophistication. On the blackboard when I visited the prison stood the French phrase *mise en place*, which was being translated as the laying out of equipment and ingredients in an orderly manner ready for the preparation of the recipe. Though prisoners could no doubt be taught by civilians from outside, the lessons help staff to feel they are making a contribution towards rehabilitation. Cooking in an institution is a possible opening upon release for some young men.

Besides, some inmates regard working in the kitchen as a privilege, but the smuggling of goods (used as currency for bartering in prison) has to be prevented, and a watch has to be kept on knives and other equipment that could be used as offensive weapons. One obvious attraction for those young prisoners on the cookery course at Aylesbury is that they can eat afterwards what they have made; this is also an incentive for good relations with staff.

Not surprisingly, the threat to prison officers' jobs and the reduction of their status has been an ingredient in the complaints bubbling at successive annual conferences of their association. Many officers feel that the Prison Service is threatened and its status undermined.

The report of the management review team is best in its diagnosis of the system, but its proposals, based on an idealised vision of relationships with prisoners as a result of the now discredited treatment philosophy, have in fact met with such resistance that the service is largely frozen in opposition even to more practical proposals.

The prison officers reacted like other minorities under threat: they felt that the very identity of the service was in danger and have become aggressive in their defence of it, overreacting to anything or anyone who fails to give them total support. That is why some of the men who have been most loyal to the discipline of the service – ex-soldiers or navy men – have been among the dissidents, something which struck members of the May Inquiry as odd.

The result has been a growth of so-called 'prison officer power', a phenomenon not unlike the growth of black power in the United States, which is also the assertion of identity against a threat, or tribal nationalisms of various kinds round the world. That is not to excuse action which has hit courts and the administration of justice hard, but, unless explanations are sought, only the symptoms, not the causes, are apparent.

Whatever merits the review team's proposals may have, they have been put forward with extraordinary clumsiness. No responsible person wishes to see trouble in prisons, where control is made that much more difficult by the nature of the prison population and years of neglect by successive governments as advised by civil servants. That is why staff set such store on the May Inquiry and expectations were raised by it, perhaps to an exaggerated extent.

The disappointment the May Inquiry Report provoked owed something to the diffidence in which parts of it were couched. The terms of reference provided by the Home Office were too narrow to enable it to deal adequately with sentencing policies (which have a direct effect on the troubles the inquiry team was exploring), yet too broad for it to examine other issues as deeply as it would have liked in the time available. One civil servant wondered if the Inquiry team knew enough about prisons to be able to examine them properly, but as the names came from the Home Office any criticism must be directed back in that direction. At times, the Report's diffidence shows signs of weakness, masquerading as a wish to be fair. The worst example is a paragraph on the appalling working conditions in many prisons:

> The increase in inmate numbers has also exacerbated already cramped conditions for staff, and we have seen for ourselves

the difficult and unsuitable circumstances in which staff may work, often without the standard of recreational and canteen facilities enjoyed in other occupations. *However soundly based the civil service rules governing the provision of such facilities (and the Department's interpretation of those rules),* these factors have further convinced prison officers that management lacks any real interest in them as people and is unconcerned with the betterment of their working environment. [The italics are mine.]

How can rules which allow such conditions possibly be soundly based? The Environmental Health Officers' Association had complained that prisons had 'Crown immunity from local authority inspections'.

It is the context and language in which the results of the inquiry are put, rather than some of the findings, which obfuscate. Inside the bureaucratic prose, strong feelings among some of the Inquiry team are struggling to get out. For example, 'scandal' is the word chosen to describe the conditions 'in which so many remand prisoners are now accommodated'. One way of tackling it, the Report says, would be to concentrate in the initial years on a programme of building adult remand accommodation. The Report chides 'successive governments' for the way in which they have responded to public concern about law and order: by steering resources towards the police as tangible evidence of their concern. 'This has both led to the relative neglect of other law and order services, notably prisons, and also increased the pressure on them of more police activity. Some witnesses commented on the need to consider law and order services more systematically and with such views we heartily concur.'

What the report does not then go on to add is that one of the arguments for siting the Prison Department within the Home Office has been to ensure that precisely that co-ordination between various services could succeed.

But what the Report does disclose is the strength with which the Home Office is prepared to defend its own position, which is in character with some of the other examples we have noted. The result is a fascinating intellectual duel between the Inquiry team and the Home Office over two issues central to one of the weaknesses disclosed in this book, many of which the May Report also charts: whether the Prison Department and its head should remain absorbed within the bureaucracy; and how independent and publicised inspections of the system should be. The argument gives further insight into the minds of highly placed civil servants.

The Home Office set out four options for the top structure of the Prison Service and its relations with the Home Office. The Inquiry Committee rejected two of them. One of those two, the minimum possible change, did little more than incorporate the much-abused Establishments Division III within the Prison Department and improve the corporate planning capacity of the Prison Board. The other would have gone even further than a resuscitated Prison Commission in its degree of complete separation from the Home Office, though the Home Secretary would have remained answerable to Parliament for its work.

The Report says: 'What we think is required is an identifiable prisons administration with clear, integrated managerial responsibility and as fully a professional operational direction as circumstances allow.'

One of the two remaining Home Office models envisaged that the Director General would become the accounting officer for all expenditure on prisons, reporting directly to the Home Secretary for the day-to-day operations and management of the service. Though the Prison Department would have its own separate establishments department, the principal establishment officer would do duty for both the Prison Department of the Home Office and for all the other departments of the latter. As such, he would report to the Director General in his former capacity and to the Permanent Under-Secretary of State (the chief civil servant at the Home Office) in the latter.

The argument in support of that option was that it would make possible the recognition of the unity and identity of purpose of staff at all grades serving in the Prison Service but nevertheless preserve for those in the general (civil service) grades opportunities for interchange with other parts of the Home Office, particularly at senior level.

One of the subjects of criticism by the May Committee was the accounting system: 'We were surprised to learn for example, that the Home Office was unable to tell us how much each prison costs to run each year. . . . We continue to feel that there must be some advantage in making the managers of institutions effectively accountable for the money that they spend.'

In the option offered to the May Inquiry there would remain a single finance department which would serve both the Prison Department and the other departments of the Home Office, but again the principal finance officer (PFO) would, like his colleague, the principle establishment officer (PEO), report to the Director General on financial matters affecting the Prison Department and to the Permanent Under-Secretary of State on financial matters relating to other departments within the Home Office. (Thus he would serve two masters, with predictable results.)

The fourth model envisaged the Prison Department having both its own PEO and PFO, with separate establishment and finance departments and responsible for all matters of staffing and finance in the Prison Service. The Committee was told that such a department, although remaining under the Home Secretary's direct control, would tend to cut off the Prison Service from the Home Office.

The May Report replies: 'We found and still find this difficult to accept.' The team is more caustic about a Home Office suggestion that, if such a model were to be adopted, then the Home Secretary would need to be provided 'with some department within the Home Office itself to advise him about the validity of advice he received from the Prison Department'.

The Report comments: 'Those of us who are less familiar with the workings of government departments than is the Permanent Under-Secretary [Sir Robert Armstrong, later Secretary to the Cabinet, one of the most powerful jobs in the Civil Service] have had considerable difficulty in reconciling ourselves to these views. . . . We do not think that the changes we propose . . . should or will have the effect of distancing the prison service in any way from the Home Office, but will merely enhance its status within it and increase its efficiency.'

The Committee explains that evidence given by the Home Office does appear 'to suggest the necessity for the creation of a separate advisory body to advise the Home Secretary, *if necessary in opposition to the Prison Department itself* [my italics], on prison matters. If this was what was intended we feel bound to

The May Inquiry

say that we cannot understand the need, far less the inevitability, of such a body. Under the arrangements which we subsequently recommend, the Home Secretary would have available to him, for advice on prison matters, both the Prison Department and HM Inspectorate of Prisons; for advice on other related matters, such as those concerned with criminal justice policy generally, he will have available to him the advice of the Permanent Under-Secretary and those who are part of whatever communication and liaison arrangements are set up, as we have mentioned. In those circumstances we can see no need for any further advisory body and we strongly express the hope that it will not be thought necessary to proliferate bureaucracies in this way.'

The Report also rejects Home Office objections to an independent inspectorate. The Home Office's opening card in the argument was that, for as long as the Prison Department remained the direct responsibility of a Minister answerable to Parliament, Parliament was the only body which had the authority to judge the quality or efficiency of the management of the Prison Service. In such circumstances 'there is no basis for an efficiency audit to be conducted by a body established so as to be independent from government'.

To that the May Inquiry retorts: 'The argument is a nice one but we think it is based upon the assumption that Parliament and government can be equated. In practice this may be so; in strict constitutional theory it is fallacious.'

The Home Office must have anticipated the Inquiry team's reply because the civil servants followed their opening card with an ace – a second and alternative argument:

If by 'independent' in this context was merely meant independent of the prison service itself and those responsible for its operational management, and it was contemplated that reports should be made direct to the Home Secretary, these, too, would not be truly independent. This was because the recipient of the reports (the Minister) and his chief lieutenant (the Permanent Under-Secretary of State) were themselves the very same people who were constitutionally responsible for the management of the prison service upon which the reports had been made. In these circumstances, the apparent independence was again illusory.

134 *Prison Crisis*

The Home Office supported its argument with one nicely tuned to catch the sympathy of a Cabinet keen to reduce cost and bureaucracy:

> If, nevertheless, that type of inspection were adopted, then there would have to be created within the Home Office some further departmental facility outside the Prison Department to advise the Permanent Under-Secretary of State whether the quasi-independent inspector's report should be accepted or not. This was because the prison service itself could not proffer that advice upon an 'independent' inspection, whether the prison service remained within or without government. The best course would be to retain the present system with a chief inspector on the Prisons Board to reinforce his substantial experience with appropriate status.

The cleverness of the Home Office argument can be judged by the fate of Brigadier Maunsell who, as we have seen, found himself as a branch of the hierarchy without twigs. On the Board, the Chief Inspector's voice is but one of several and his freedom can be curtailed. The terms of reference for the investigation by Mr Fowler, then Chief Inspector, of the Hull riot meant that he could not examine the principal allegations against prison officers. Part of the pressure on officers everywhere comes as a result of the way the Home Office system operates. But, in an apparent concession to the May Inquiry, the Home Office agreed that the Inspector's words might well be incorporated in that year's report on the work of the Prison Department, and so wide circulation would be given to more general comments, good or bad.

However, the Home Office's annual report on prisons has not always been the most detailed of documents. The full report on the Parkhurst trouble has never been published – only a small item tucked away in the following year's report. And, in 1979, the investigation by a senior prison official, chosen from within the department, of prisoners' allegations against officers in Wormwood Scrubs was not intended for publication. Mr Whitelaw instead promised to make a statement.

The Home Office argued in evidence to the May Inquiry that the Chief Inspector's reports should not be published because they might well contain 'frank criticisms of personal performances which it would be better to keep within the sphere of management and not make available to a larger audience'. (Thus does the Home Office disclose how, by secrecy, it is prepared to shield public officials from public scrutiny.)

Against these arguments, the May Committee played their trump – the need for more open government (publicly professed by the Home Office) and the need to keep control over the executive (which was mentioned in the Conservatives' manifesto before they came to power and has since been dramatised by the spy scandal involving Anthony Blunt).

The May Committee's trump was:

> We need have no doubt both that the prison service would benefit from, and that public sentiment requires that, as many aspects of government, which includes the prison service, should be opened up to as wide an audience as possible. We therefore think that there should be a system of inspection of the prison service which, although not 'independent' of it in either of the senses canvassed in the Home Office paper, should nevertheless be distanced from it as far as may be practicable.

The May Report says that regional directors should carry out the in-depth inspections of particular establishments hitherto carried out by the Chief Inspector and his department, as part of operational management duties. Their job would not, for example, include looking at the trouble at Wormwood Scrubs, the method for which has caused much criticism. For that sort of investigation the May Inquiry suggests another way:

> We do, however, recommend that there should be constituted within the Home Office an independent department to be called the 'prison inspectorate', headed either by someone independent of the civil service entirely or by a senior ex-governor as the Home Secretary may decide.
> The post should be of HM Chief Inspector of Prisons, holding the rank between that of Deputy and Assistant Under-Secretary of State. [The reason for this will be seen later.] The Department should not be a big one, but it should contain people with

relevant prison service experience as well as such others as the Home Secretary thinks appropriate.

HM Chief Inspector of Prisons and his staff should be available to make *ad hoc* inspections of any incidents which may occur, at the request of the Home Secretary; they should be empowered to set out unannounced and make an inspection of a particular establishment or a particular part of an establishment as and when they think it necessary or desirable to do so; they should also make inspections of more general aspects of the work of the prison service – for instance, of accounting procedures, or into questions of quarters, or into particular aspects of security or control. We recommend that, except where security considerations dictate otherwise, the reports of HM Chief Inspector of Prisons should be published and laid before Parliament and that each year his department should also make a general report on the whole prison service, insofar as they have seen it during the year, which should be included in that year's report of the work of the prison department.

The argument set out by the May team led to its recommendation that the Prison Service should have a greater degree of autonomy within the Home Office than at present.

The Inquiry team said that there was no evidence suggesting the need for substantial change in the organisation of the prison services in Scotland and Northern Ireland. The Home Secretary should remain accountable to Parliament for the running of the Prison Service in England and Wales. Central administration ought to have shown itself more responsive to growing feelings of dissatisfaction with the organisation and management of the service as a whole, especially in the field of personnel management.

Establishments Division III should be absorbed within the Prison Department, the Report says. The Prison Department should have a reliable view of comparative unit costs of its operation and be capable of developing financial controls which enhance efficiency and managerial performance. Governors must be capable of having proper regard to the efficiency and economic use of public resources.

The Prison Service should be reorganised with a view, first, to creating within it a greater degree of unity and identity than at present exists; second, to giving the Prison Department more standing within the Home Office; and third, to identifying those areas of its administration and work which should be the concern and responsibility of the most senior management. The affairs of Her Majesty's Prison Service in England and Wales should continue to be directed by a Prisons Board. The Prisons Board should be headed by a chairman, who would be the accounting officer for the Prison Service, with direct access to the Home Secretary, and who should be of Second Permanent Secretary rank. (By use of the words 'Her Majesty's', the Inquiry team, whether consciously or not, emphasises that Prison Service is not a fief of the Civil Service, and the rank of Second Permanent Secretary is intended to give the head of the service enough status to be able to withstand pressure from it. The need for direct access to the Home Secretary speaks for itself.)

The Report adds that the chairman should be a career civil servant, an ex-governor, or someone from outside the Civil Service. He should remain in post for at least five, and preferably seven, years. He should be someone with the high administrative qualities required and also such knowledge and experience of government as would enable him to fight for, obtain, and administer the resources for the service which are vital.

The report says that the Prisons Board should include a further six members, four of whom should originate either from the general Civil Service or the governor grades. The first, the deputy chairman and director of operations should hold a rank between that of Deputy and Assistant Under-Secretary of State (the same as that recommended for the Inspector General), but the others should be of the rank of Assistant Under-Secretary of State. Ordinarily, he should be the most suitable former member of the governor grades. It would be to him that press, television and radio would look first for statements and explanations about anything and everything that might occur in the field in the Prison Service. Others on the Board would be the Director of Personnel, Director of Regimes and Director of Finance and Administration. In addition there should be two entirely independent non-executive members, appointed by the Home Secretary.

Under the Report's recommendations, the much vilified Establishments Division III would come under the Director of Personnel and it would probably be desirable to have a separate principal finance officer under the director of finance and administration in a new centre to control all financial affairs.

So far as Scotland is concerned, the May Committee criticised the fact that the statutory provision of visiting committees for adult establishments in Scotland (appointed by the local authorities of the area in which the establishment was located) had not been amended following the reform of local government in Scotland in 1975. The Report says: 'Immediate steps should be taken to secure the necessary statutory authority to regularise the position of visiting committees for adult establishments in Scotland.'

The Committee also criticised the lack of formal training for visiting committees and recommended that immediate steps should be taken to ensure that proper training, instruction and information should be given to all members of the committees.

May recommended that Peterhead Prison should be substantially developed on the ample site available, especially if Shotts Prison was not to be used, in part, to replace it; and the Shotts project should be restored.

2 DEALING WITH THE PRISONS

Apart from some pussy-footing about the aspirations of the bureaucracy, the May Report included some succinct conclusions and recommendations which, if acted upon, would do much to reduce some of the pressure on the prison system. The value of the Report is marked more by its bringing together suggestions already current in the penological field than by bold new initiatives. There is, for example, little new about its suggestion that successful attempts to reduce inmate populations in Holland and Sweden indicate that UK practices, especially sentencing policy, require reexamination. Academics and others in the penological field have been doing little else for the past ten years.

Lord Butler's Committee and others concerned with mental health had condemned the failure of the DHSS to care for people sick in mind who have thus to stay in prison. But an unequivocal statement by the May Inquiry that 'the DHSS should take urgent steps to ensure that the NHS lives up to its proper responsibilities in respect of them' will strengthen the hand of the Home Office for interdepartmental in-fighting.

As would many concerned with the fate of petty offenders, the May Committee wants more treatment of them in the community, adding that prison should be avoided wherever possible for fine and maintenance defaulters as well as for drunkenness. More determination, it says, should be shown in dealing with alcoholism and local voluntary schemes should be encouraged.

The Committee merely says of executive intervention through remission schemes and parole that it should be kept under consideration, but does not produce a strong recommendation of its own.

The road to hell in prison for inmates and staff is paved with the good intentions of committees, and May has a shot at producing some new aims to replace the existing Rule 1 of the Prison Rules: 'The purpose of the training and treatment of convicted prisoners shall be to encourage and assist them to lead a good and useful life.' Out of Rule 1 has sprung much rhetoric about treatment and training; the Committee quite rightly wishes to replace the rhetoric but not 'all the admirable and constructive things that are done in its name'.

The Committee's own suggestions for a new Rule 1 are more banal and less inspiring than the original, though they serve some purpose in spelling out what it means by 'positive custody', which May has evolved as an aim. Certainly it is more constructive than 'humane containment' as an ideal, but it lacks nobility of language that can ring in the hearts and minds of prison staff:

> The purpose of the detention of convicted prisoners shall be to keep them in custody which is both secure and yet positive, and to that end the behaviour of all the responsible authorities and staff towards them shall be such as to:
> (a) create an environment which can assist them to respond and contribute to society as positively as possible;
> (b) preserve and promote their self-respect;
> (c) minimise, to the degree of security necessary in each particular case, the harmful effects of their removal from normal life;
> (d) prepare them for and assist them on discharge.

The aims, which have the dubious merit of avoiding offence, will no doubt receive the academic attention they deserve: they will also provide fruitful grounds for dispute by prison-cell lawyers.

The real weakness of the Committee's language is that the first sentence of the new rule is too long for anyone to be able to remember. Indeed, the whole rule consists of only one sentence – of ninety-three words.

Quite rightly, the Committee stresses the importance of the role of boards of visitors, recognising the need to care for the welfare of staff and their families as well as inmates. One worthwhile idea in the Report is that boards should also be encouraged to do more to involve their prison and its community, staff and inmates, in the local community.

Nor does it shirk demanding of the Lord Chancellor's Department that it pay for time-consuming escort and dock-manning duties by staff on an agency basis, so as to encourage both it and the Home Office to save manpower. The Committee suggests that the amount of overtime being worked – good neither for the service nor for staff and families – raises questions about the efficient use of manpower. It urges a single attendance system for prison officers in England and Wales, which should conform to certain specified criteria. There should, in any case, be a thorough review of working methods, it says.

Evidence of the appalling state of prisons also leads the Inquiry team to say:

> The worst prisons are very bad indeed, but the worst are not always Victorian prisons. Dartmoor prison should be closed and Peterhead prison [in Scotland] should be substantially redeveloped.
>
> Acceptable modern standards – for the staff as for inmates – require that the European and the United Nations Standard minimum rules should be interpreted in the UK as requiring a minimum target of eliminating enforced cell sharing and incorporating integral sanitation not only in all new prisons but in all redeveloped or substantially improved accommodation.

Most important, the Committee is not in favour of concentrating Category A prisoners rather than dispersing them, as is done at present, although the present system has contributed towards disturbances.

The Report concludes that expenditure on prisons in England and Wales has not invariably compared unfavourably with selected social services and total public expenditure. But expenditure on prisons, because of its small volume, has suffered disproportionately from successive cuts in expenditure plans :

> Plans should be drawn up for new prison building programmes in England and Wales and Scotland aimed at both eliminating cell sharing other than in dormitories or specially enlarged cells and at producing integral sanitation and washing facilities progressively throughout prison establishments. No programme can be credible which does not deal with the Victorian local prisons. In England and Wales this will entail approximately doubling present capital expenditure

The Report suggests concentrating initial effort on adult remand accommodation and ending 'the scandal of the conditions in which so many remand prisoners are held'. But it is regrettable that the May Committee is not in favour of more money being made available for probation.

The Committee is on the side of many prison officers who wish to extend their role and to undertake a wider range of duties. It says that existing experiments in which prison officers undertake wider duties (some of them have been mentioned in this book) should be extended to other establishments. And greater consideration should be given to involving prison officers, on secondment, with a range of activities outside penal establishments. Greater involvement of local volunteers and community groups outside should be encouraged in appropriate activities within establishments.

But it also says that prison officers should take a more flexible approach than hitherto to manning levels and attendance systems, and should accept that there are a number of tasks within penal establishments which do not require the skills, experience and training of prison officers.

Though chief officers feel that the Report in its recommendations does not go far enough towards enhancing their status, not least by way of pay, the Inquiry team says: 'It is essential that the importance of the rank of chief officer should be fully recognised by junior officers and by senior management alike.'

The Report says that comparison with earnings generally showed that junior prison grades stood well – and even better if free housing, free uniform and non-contributory pension were considered in addition – in comparison with average gross earnings, but worked longer than average hours to do so. There was no evidence to show that they had lost any real ground recently. Since officers' gross earnings compare well, a large increase in basic pay is not justified, the Report says. But pay should be increased with effect from 1 January 1980 to newly recommended levels over those originally agreed in order to reflect the more difficult control problems since 1958 and the need to recruit more officers.

The rises include some special increases and the introduction of a modest incremental scale for chief officers, as well as two long-service increments for basic-grade officers. The Report says that, while the consolidation of certain allowances into basic pay could not now be justified, the parties should address their minds to the question of consolidation. Provocatively, however, the Report says that the inconvenience of locality allowances should be phased out by negotiation. (Parkhurst's demands for extra special allowances for living on the Isle of Wight led, of course, to long-running industrial action.)

Saying that training needs to have more priority to make it effective, the Report foresees the need for governors to consult staff and resolve disputes locally where possible. There is a corresponding need, the Report says, for staff to accept that issues must be decided on merit, not by reference to practice elsewhere. (The effect of these proposals would be an emphasis on decentralisation, which would help to reduce the too great power at present held in Whitehall.)

Showing awareness of the vulnerability of staff to malicious allegations, the Report says that consideration should be given to renegotiation of the code of discipline. It speaks also of the need to avoid any suspicion of oversensitivity by staff to external investigation. Much will obviously depend on how much the proposals in the Report can create a climate of confidence. At least it shows concern for the welfare of officers in urging improvement in their working facilities, such as better toilets, office accommodation, showers and places for clothes drying. 'Prison establishments should be open to inspection by HM Factory Inspectors, Public Health

Inspectors and similar officials to the same extent as any private establishment.'

But on the issues which caused officers particular concern when they took industrial action – claims for payment in respect of meal breaks taken within duty hours – the May Inquiry has done little to cool the anger within the service. A national agreement in general requires officers to work net hours; that is to say that they receive payment only for hours actually worked and do not receive payment for any meal breaks which fall within the normal span of their working shift unless that is expressly provided for either by agreement or by a provision in the codes regulating their systems of attendance. The Report says: 'In the absence of any such provision the general rule about non-payment for meal breaks must, in our opinion, prevail.'

The May Committee, however, did not adopt the basic principle that prison officers should have roughly what they have now in total income, without working so many hours for it and without the crazily complicated allowances system. There would therefore have to be some hard bargaining to secure realistic manning levels, instead of the inflated ones which always allow the claim that establishment is under strength and officers must be called in for overtime.

Chapter 12

Rescuing the Prisons

The remedies suggested by the May Inquiry do not go far enough, partly because the narrowness of the terms of reference did not allow the Committee adequately to consider sentencing policy.

SENTENCING

Before suggesting ways in which the prison population could be cut, it is necessary to see where the rises have been most significant. Since 1947, the average daily population has increased by nearly two and a half times, but the number of remand prisoners has increased more than fourfold. That is partly the result of increased numbers received into custody, but is also partly due to the increased average time such prisoners are held on remand (often in scandalous conditions).

The figure is evidence of the inefficiency of processing cases through courts and the need for more resources. Police and other witnesses frequently complain of the length of time taken before cases are heard, which dims recollection of evidence, and of the arbitrary way in which they are kept hanging about outside courtrooms, waiting to be called.

All remand prisoners should be regarded as still the general responsibility of the Lord Chancellor's Department. Only when they have been sentenced to custody, probation or one of the other forms of disposal under the Home Office wing should they be regarded as under its general overall responsibility (though of course it would still have the job of providing humane custody for remand prisoners.)

The May Inquiry team has suggested that the Lord Chancellor's Department should pay for escorts. The logical extension of that idea is that his Department should also pay for the stay in prison of those people who have still to be found guilty or sentenced. The payment would be an incentive to the Department to improve the speed with which cases are brought to court.

More money should also be spent on bail hostels. The Home Office in November 1979 gave a figure of only 24 hostels – both bail and probation hostels – in the 56 probation areas of England and Wales, with only 360 places. The figure does not differentiate between the two categories and is appallingly low, given the propensity of courts to remand in custody people of no settled abode.

In the last thirty years the smallest proportion in the rise of receptions was of people who form the largest section of the population – those sentenced to immediate imprisonment. But receptions of fine defaulters increased more than fivefold. The options at present open to courts for fine defaulters are too few. Courts are loath to use distraint orders to make defaulters forfeit goods or to order an employer to make a deduction from pay. Imprisonment is an option if there is culpable neglect or refusal to pay but the court can order a means test.

As the Howard League pointed out in its May 1974 Newsletter, the Wootton Committee in 1970 on Non-Custodial and Semi-Custodial Penalties recommended unanimously that 'non-custodial penalties should be truly non-custodial . . . offenders upon whom a fine has been imposed should not be committed to prison if they have failed' to pay.

The League said that magistrates continued to fine destitute offenders such as vagrant alcoholics and beggars, and then imprison them for failure to pay. As a result, many were sent to already overfull prisons for offences – like simple drunkenness – which were not even punishable by imprisonment.

While some 20 per cent of imprisoned offenders did secure their release by prompt payment, a far larger group did not: over 60 per cent (6,300 out of 10,300 in 1972) served more than half their sentences, the League said.

The largest group who did not buy their liberty were those with sentences not exceeding one month – the petty offenders.

Over two-thirds of the 3,600 defaulters who in 1972 served over 80 per cent of their sentences were charged with non-indictable offences. Drunkenness figured prominently among them. More than half of the offenders imprisoned in default of drunkenness fines had been refused time to pay.

Since the 1967 Criminal Justice Act required the courts to give offenders time to pay, except in specified cases, it could be assumed that many who were refused time were 'of no fixed abode' – homeless and destitute vagrants. Not surprisingly, the vast majority served more than 80 per cent of their sentences. The same was true of the smaller number of offenders who were imprisoned for failing to pay fines for begging and sleeping out.

Though prison acts as an asylum for people like these, particularly in winter, the League said: 'We believe that action should be taken without delay to implement the Wootton Committee's recommendation. Certainly accommodation is needed for these destitute people – but not in prisons. Poverty is a social problem and it should cease to be an imprisonable offence.'

The League added that every year over 3,000 men were imprisoned by magistrates' courts because they had defaulted in the payment of maintenance to their wives or children.

Since they did not pay, neither their families nor the Department of Health and Social Security were better off. Nor was imprisonment a deterrent to the defaulter. All the studies showed that recidivism was to be expected. The Payne Committee, which reported on the issue did not think that fear of jail was needed 'in order to deter the generality of husbands from neglect of their familial obligations'. The League added: 'We agree with this view. If a maintenance defaulter has the means to pay, an efficient machinery of extraction should ensure that the money reaches his dependants. But imprisonment as a means of extracting money has now – by the official figures – been shown to be a complete failure. We therefore believe that the time has come to abolish the imprisonment of maintenance defaulters. It does no good and much harm.'

Community service should be made available in many cases as another option for fine defaulting, though not to the extent that the system would be in danger of breaking down. The logic for its use is that people have to pay fines out of their income. But if they default, through being out of work or through fecklessness if working, they should be given the chance of volunteering for employment on community service for an appropriate number of hours work, to 'earn' roughly the equivalent of the fine.

The largest proportionate increase in numbers of people received was in young people sent to borstals or detention centres. The reason given by some chief probation officers is that juvenile courts are becoming increasingly reluctant to place children in the care of local authorities. (The May Committee pointed out that the detention centre population grew as places became available. The population of detention centres and borstals might have grown still more if places had been available. The question is: Why?)

Before the 1969 Children and Young Persons Act came into force, juvenile courts could commit youngsters to approved schools. The equivalent nowadays is to place them into care, perhaps with a recommendation, but many magistrates say they have lost confidence in the ability of social work departments to oversee the best course for them. Thus, to make sure the public are protected from the depredations of recidivist young people, courts try to make sure they are locked up in borstals and detention centres.

If magistrates in juvenile courts received the power to sentence young people 14–16 to what was felt to be the most appropriate disposal, including secure accommodation in a home, they could adopt a more flexible approach. But shortage of places remains a problem. If money was given to the Probation Service to provide them, the government would at least be certain that it would go to the purpose intended. More use of foster homes could also be a possibility.

The Probation Service has responsibility only for those aged seventeen and older. Social workers are, in theory, supposed to deal with juveniles, but in many cases probation officers already act for them. Probation officers should also be given the job of supervising 14–16-year-olds on the grounds that children in that age group know the difference between right and wrong, that penal sanctions will help to emphasise it, and that more status should be returned to the courts.

Because sixteen-year-olds do not appear before adult courts they cannot be given community service orders or other options more suitable than at present available. That should be changed, but they should not be treated wholly as young adults and sentences of imprisonment should not be available except in cases where they can already be used, though more imagination should be given to the use of imprisonment when it is justified and to regimes.

Perhaps prematurely, the Howard League says in the *Howard Journal*:

> Happily there seems now to be almost universal agreement that Secure Care Orders are not a practicable possibility. Juvenile court magistrates, smarting under their supposed loss of powers under the 1969 Children and Young Persons Act, for some time campaigned for the power to make such an order, and at the 1976 annual general meeting of the Magistrates' Association a resolution was passed with only four dissentient votes.

The League claims that the objections to a secure care order are 'enormous'. Most importantly, it goes on, such an order would be anti-therapeutic because even with the best possible advice no court is in a position to assess the length of time during which a youngster is likely to need secure containment, and to keep him or her locked up for a day more than is necessary may cause considerable emotional damage. The shortage of qualified residential staff who can provide the care as well as the security adds to the risk.

Many of the children come from disturbed home backgrounds, or are homeless: putting them into institutions merely delays the time when these problems have to be tackled. (The criteria for placing youngsters in secure conditions have been analysed in the Howard League report in 1971, *'Unruly' Children in a human context*.)

The second objection, the League says, is one of priorities. Secure accommodation is (thankfully) in short supply and no court is in a position to assess the needs of a particular child in relation to those who have been before them in the past, will come before them in the future, or indeed may demonstrate a need for some form of security without ever appearing before a court. The League adds: 'A Secure Care Order would therefore result in the use of a scarce resource in an inefficient manner.'

There speaks the authentic voice of liberal enlightenment, the fruit of 200 years of reforming zeal, and long may it continue. But the 1969 Children and Young Persons Act saw the zenith, at least temporarily, of that movement; and practical politicians have also to think of the art of the possible. The sad fact is that the present system is not working and there is an overwhelmingly powerful argument for returning power to the magistrates, partly for reasons we dealt with earlier: particularly because of the need for participation of the members of the public, through the magistracy (as through the jury) in a penal system which would otherwise be even more remote and elitist than it is already. Magistrates should be given back powers in respect of this issue, though it may well be that appropriate safeguards are needed so that misuse of that power does not occur. There is a stronger case for another idea put forward by the Howard League – the use of restitution orders.

In prison most people are serving sentences at the shorter end of the scale. Seventy-six per cent of the population are doing 18 months or less and 95 per cent up to four years. For some of them a police caution might be more appropriate. Increasing use should be made of probation, which has a good record. The extra responsibilities of probation officers means that more should be recruited and some resources moved to them from the Prison Department, with suitable prison officers temporarily transferred to work with the Probation Service to develop their skills in rehabilitation.

There should be greater clarity of language and purpose in sentencing, otherwise people are likely to be confused about its true meaning. (Court hearings are already full enough of mumbo-jumbo.) The life sentence is an example. 'Life' does not mean what it says, and should be replaced with determinate sentences which would put greater responsibility on the courts. Equally important, the change would reduce the power of the executive and help to remove at least some of the uncertainty that lifers feel. Criminals who would previously have been sentenced to life should have their cases reviewed by the Parole Board, but be released on licence, not parole, with the possibility of recall at any time in their lives, should it be necessary. It is possible to put into a different category abnormal prisoners who have not lost the urge to kill, and treat them under the Mental Health Acts, revised where necessary, so that they do not emerge until it is safe for them to do so. That process should be subject, of course, to safeguards for the prisoner. More accommodation should be made available in NHS psychiatric and semi-secure units to relieve pressure on special hospitals like Broadmoor.

PRISON ADMINISTRATION

It should be the aim as far as possible to give prisoners services as they are available in the outside world. For example, the National Health Service should take over the provision of medical care in prisons and pay the Home Office a fee for the accommodation of those who should be in hospital. The Home Office argument against that is that posts in some prisons, being remote, would not attract doctors if they were transferred to the National Health Service. The argument is fallacious. National Health doctors already cover remote areas in general practice. The Home Office is at present not very good at attracting recruits. Pay is obviously a factor. If doctors were given a greater incentive to work in prisons, it would be more possible to attract recruits, whether the system were under the National Health Service or not.

There is an even greater reason for doctors to be employed by the National Health Service: to avoid any suspicions that some doctors use their skills as part of the control process.

Allowing a person in prison to be visited by his own National Health Service doctor would help to increase his confidence in treatment. There would then be absolutely no doubt that a doctor's first responsibility was to his patient and not Whitehall. A similar argument applies to chaplains and their flock.

Generally, administration needs to be modernised so that a daily tally can be made easily of available accommodation throughout the system and communications greatly improved. Telex machines should be installed in every establishment. Sir Derek Rayner, joint managing director of Marks and Spencer and the Prime Minister's adviser on the elimination of government waste, should be invited to apply his talents to the Prison Service to reduce paperwork. Administration should be streamlined and responsibilities divided clearly so that staff feel a greater sense of them and know precisely what their duties entail. (An example of potential difficulty is the division of responsibility between junior assistant governors and chief prison officers. Having served as a junior pilot officer in the RAF, I know that the answer in that particular case is use of common sense; no junior pilot officer in his right mind would pretend to know more about routine than the station warrant officer, but a fusion of the warrant officer's experience and know-how and the young officer's bright ideas, if he had any, could be to the good of the service.)

Daily the latest figures of available accommodation in prisons should be available to courts, broken down into appropriate categories, for their general guidance. A precedent has already been set with detention centres. Before people can be sent to them justices' clerks have to make sure places are available. Courts should not be so formally restricted in the case of other establishments, as they must retain the freedom to choose what they think to be the most appropriate sentence in particular cases. But a spell in an overcrowded prison might not be appropriate if proper attention could not be given to the prisoner. Giving figures of available accommodation to courts would help them to judge if it was humanly possible to give treatment of the kind proposed by a particular kind of sentence. (By treatment in this sense I mean whether the regime available would allow the prisoner to be kept in custody in the way desired by the court.)

Courts should also bear in mind the availability of accommodation when deciding on length of sentence. Proposals to reduce sentences should be introduced in the middle and lower end of the scale, while retaining for serious crimes of violence, spying and offences such as drug trafficking the option of heavier sentences which would emphasise the severity with which such behaviour is viewed by the court and the public. But the arguments already outlined in publications on sentencing should be rewritten more convincingly. There has been a failure to communicate adequately the need for shorter sentences in appropriate cases, about which there is more agreement than is always apparent.

More encouragement should be given to present experiments being done in the field of intermediate treatment, not least by the probation service and NACRO. Some include a 'package' of treatment of various sorts for the individual offences. That is a welcome recognition that a blanket, uniform philosophy of penal treatment, in the latest fashion, is not suitable for all the many different kinds of offender in each category. The real merit of experiment is to widen the range of options, so that they can be employed more flexibly and to suit the offender. It may be that one offender on a wing wishes to get down and 'do his bird' (meaning serve his sentence) without aggravation, revelling in simply being contained humanely, however negative the philosophy would be if applied uniformly throughout the system. Yet an apathetic prisoner on the same wing might suddenly become enthused by the help of a prison officer to some new attainment. It is moving to see 'life' prisoners in Portsmouth Prison who have benefited from the encouragement given them by staff: one had just learnt to read and write, though middle-aged, and could for the first time understand the letters sent in by his family; another had been given encouragement by an officer in the making and painting of model soldiers, which, when done properly, can form a collection of some value.

STAFF

Present arrangements do not always permit officers to get to know prisoners well, because staff are not always long enough on the same landings. As at Hull, lack of contact – and therefore knowledge – can be dangerous. Like policemen, officers should be restored to a regular beat.

It remains to be seen whether the May Committee's recommendations on pay, which the Home Secretary, Mr William Whitelaw, immediately accepted, will be able to attract recruits of sufficient calibre and in sufficient numbers. The suspicion remains that they will not, although first signs are encouraging. The Committee evidently thought that living in a tied house belonging to the Prison Department was a benefit, though most people today would wish to invest in house purchase as a hedge against inflation.

Prison officers gave notice that as from a date in January 1980 they would not be bound by orders to do overtime, though it was still open to governors of establishments to ask them to do it and for them to accept, and one governor was quick to reach a local agreement with his men so as to cover duties.

Those officers willing to do overtime may well have to stay at the prison for their meals, so as to enable them to continue with their extra duties. On the issue of meal breaks the May Committee should have given more attention to considering whether natural justice was being done on the broad issue. If officers are asked to do overtime, they should eat in their dining-room or in the club on the premises so as to be immediately available in case of emergency. In this, they are unlike most civil servants.

Since meals are taken as part of their stay on the premises, they may be unable to pop home during their break, and even if they could they would still not be able to relax fully, knowing that they must be keyed up and alert in what is a peculiarly demanding job. They should therefore receive recompense for those meal breaks. But adequate control should be exercised by chief officers to ensure that paid meal breaks are taken only when absolutely necessary.

The Committee has also gone only an insufficient part of the way towards changing the emphasis away from rewards for long hours towards rewards for merit, skill and experience. It is recognised that training is inadequate, but important extra training successfully completed deserves extra money. Even boy scouts get badges for gaining particular skills and knowledge; some recognition should be given to better trained officers. Extra pay is not a sufficient incentive by itself though. Greater recognition needs to be accorded at high level to courage, endurance and the exercise of restraint, skill and discipline beyond the call of duty in the most trying of circumstances. Much has been heard of officers' bad behaviour at various incidents and too little recognition been given to the good. Too few prison staff figure in honours lists. A special new medal should also be made available for staff who deserve it for exceptional devotion to duty, and the Queen invited to present it. Such recognition would do something to help officers realise that there is public appreciation of their worth and increase their self-esteem and loyalty to the service.

Similarly, greater pay differentials should be given to senior staff, whether at officer or governor grade, not least when senior uniformed staff transfer to the grade. Arrangements should be made to train governors better for the highest posts in the service. The Government should publicly declare its intention of making an ex-governor Chairman of the Prison Board within a fixed time, say seven years. That would provide an incentive to find and train suitable candidates from within the service.

BOARDS OF VISITORS

The position of boards of visitors must be strengthened, so that their influence on what happens in prisons is greater. They are appointed by the Home Secretary to keep an eye on prisons. The Home Office says that they constitute an independent body of representatives of the local community to which an inmate may make a complaint or request both at their regular meetings . . . and during visits which individual members make.

The boards are also at present the superior disciplinary authority, adjudicating when inmates are charged with relatively serious offences against discipline.

The two roles should be separated, as suggested by a committee set up by Justice, the Howard League for Penal Reform and the National Association for the Care and Resettlement of Offenders, and chaired by Earl Jellicoe. Serious offences against discipline should be tried by professional adjudicators drawn from lawyers of the standing required for appointment as circuit judges or recorders. The professional chairman should sit with two lay magistrates.

The Jellicoe Committee said that, as a supervisory body, a board of visitors should enjoy and display 'conspicuous independence and it should do so primarily by being divorced from executive responsibility of any kind. It should be extremely well informed, have no axes to grind, and be an utterly frank and constructive adviser.' But in the last resort, responsibility must rest with the Prisons Board and the Home Secretary.

There should be a national council of boards of visitors, however, to strengthen the hand of individual members, who may feel under pressure from inmates, staff or even the Home Office, in doing a job diligently. Some members of boards are already pressing to form a national body, and should receive encouragement to do so.

The work of such bodies would supplement inspections done by the professionals in the Prison Service by helping to ensure that findings made by them were properly implemented. The board could also act as a watchdog to alert the professional inspector if things in an establishment were going wrong. The boards should take more responsibility for the welfare of staff and their families.

There should be five independent members of the Prisons Board, not two, and one of them, representing the public interest, should be the chairman of the national council of boards. Another should be a chief probation officer, so as to ensure proper liaison between the two services. Representatives of the TUC and CBI should be included to liaise over obtaining jobs for prisoners after release. Each board should produce its own independent annual report about the state of the prison it supervises. The reports would be public documents and would contribute to debate about prisons, thus helping to put them higher on the national agenda, exposing any malpractice and making what is, after all, a public service more accountable to the public. The national council should produce each year a commentary on the Prison Department's annual report, to be published as part of it, drawing on the reports of local boards.

PAY FOR PRISONERS

Prisoners should be given opportunity to earn enough money to pay for the upkeep of their families, rather than leaving them to rely on social security. Wages should be high enough to replace social security, so as to enable him or her to make a new start in life. It would mean a simple transfer of payments from one source to another and would cost the country little more – a small price to pay for helping to motivate people to keep out of trouble and feel a sense of responsibility to the families which would have to look to the state anyway in most cases. Prisoners in solitary confinement of their own volition (because, for example, of victimisation by other prisoners) should also be given work to keep them occupied. But those there for punishment should not, though some limited opportunities for association should be allowed under strict supervision to avoid sensory deprivation. For their families money should come from social security payments; prisoners' wages should be higher than them to be an incentive.

The money for the upkeep of the prisoner's family should be retained by the authorities and sent to them. The prison authorities should also set aside money to be kept for the prisoner on release, so that he has no immediate need for recourse to social security. Only a small amount, the same as now, should be available for the prisoners while inside. The reason for that is experience gained in Denmark. One prison officer there showed me his wage-slip and complained: 'After all my outgoings, prisoners have more pocket-money than I do.'

FAMILY CONTACTS

There should be no conjugal rights for prisoners while they are in prison. Experience in more liberal Denmark shows that once wives had been admitted so that sexual intercourse could take place it was difficult not to extend the privilege to fiancées and 'steady' girl friends. A prison officer told me of unofficial arrangements whereby, for payment of £19, a prostitute could be brought into the prison from Copenhagen's 'red light' district.

But contacts with families should be preserved as far as possible by relaxing censorship in Category C prisons and restrictions on correspondence more generally. Where questions of security are not involved there should be access to a telephone, and, particularly towards the end of a sentence, more home leaves.

SECRECY

The 1979 annual report of the Prison Department gave franker and more complete coverage of the year's events than was the case in previous years.

But there still remains a defensiveness behind the Prison Department's apparent willingness to go along with the new policy of openness. Some journalists still find difficulty in getting into prisons when there has been, or is, trouble, though it is understandable that the authorities should be concerned about control. But what prisoner would regard it as in his or her interest to be delinquent in front of a reporter or a television camera (unless he or she was so abnormal as to lose self-control)?

Generally the Official Secrets Act should not cover prisons, though it should be retained for control of information only about the most sensitive details of a prison's security system. There should also remain a general bar on giving details about individual prisoners, although they should be able to identify themselves before or in the media if they wish and speak to reporters. Staff already do this through membership of their unions about matters that can be fairly said to do with pay and working conditions. But, just as Sir Robert Mark, when Commissioner of the Metropolitan Police, allowed more senior officers to give interviews to the media, so the Prison Department should allow senior prison staff. And proper training should be given for that.

A NEW RULE

Prisons today lack hope and inspiration. The Victorian ideals provided a goal that has since vanished with the erosion of faith. Yet the ideas of repentance and redemption have underpinned western values for two thousand years. It was natural that such ideas should be strong in prison, 'place of sinners'. Whatever one thinks about Christianity and what has been done in its name, prisoners were not viewed mechanistically, though they were treated harshly physically by today's standards.

It was from those beliefs that Rule 1 evolved eventually in its present form: 'The purpose of the training and treatment of convicted prisoners shall be to encourage and assist them to lead a good and useful life.' The spirit of redemption is there, although the rule begs questions. It imposes a responsibility on those able to help, but at most it is a compassionate educative role that has been given the service, important though that is. It stands well, for example, beside the idea of 'humane containment', a sterile concept which, by itself, would reduce prison officers to zoo-keepers. The idea of 'just deserts', also discussed in penological circles, implies that a person gets what he or she deserves for the crime committed and it hints more at retribution than redemption. Few people are wholly bad: one can see that in the toys that prisoners make for children at Christmas or the braille on which prisoners at Aylesbury work so diligently for the benefit of the blind. Sometimes prisoners feel the need for atonement.

Rule 1 must be simple and make a general point, simply because it is Rule 1 and therefore all else springs from it. Also, people in prisons and involved with them must be able to remember it and make sense of it and use it as guidance. The Rule 1 suggested by the May Committee unfortunately takes a total of ninety-three words, all in one hideous sentence, to explain. 'Purposive custody' is the shorthand used for it; but then, all custody has to be purposive, even if the purpose is only 'humane containment'.

With all these thoughts in mind I have adapted a verse from the Gospel According to St Luke, from the King James Bible: 'The purpose of imprisonment is to help turn the disobedient to the wisdom of the just.'

The word 'disobedient' implies that the law has been broken by the prisoner, but it could equally well be applied to the erring officer. The sentence implies that behind the law, however, there are deeper values which it articulates and which are expressed through 'the wisdom of the just'. It is a rule that can be applied by any officer of whatever rank, because it places a responsibility on him to be wise and just, so that the disobedient may respect him for his bearing and character and not just his toughness, though people have to be tough with themselves to remain wise and just under provocation. Discipline within the Prison Service, enhanced by the respect given to the chief officer, who should be the embodiment of wisdom and justice, helps to create the mood of strength through restraint which must be the hallmark of quality within prisons. Such a rule could be applied more generally. For example, it would be unjust and unwise to imprison mental patients instead of treating them in hospitals. Such a rule would put a heavy responsibility on both lawmakers and law enforcers; yet already there are people who fulfil that quality. At his best, Lord Denning is the outstanding example of a wise and just man.

For the prisoner, there is a need to recognise that he has been 'disobedient'. The best prison officers can spot the moment when a man who has murdered is ready to come to terms with himself and society: it is when he has experienced remorse; in other words, after he has recognised the extent of his disobedience, pleading guilty to himself.

It is then that the prison officer can try to turn him or her to the wisdom of the just. For the phrase 'the wisdom of the just' can also imply the collective values of society that have been handed down over generations – values the law seeks to uphold. They are older than Christianity and, since prisons are about morality, as much attention needs to be paid to history and philosophy as to criminology and sociology, which otherwise lack meaning by existing in a moral vacuum. As Dante wrote,

> Ye were not born to live the lives of brutes
> But virtue to pursue and knowledge high.

Once the renewed values I recommend had been recognised in the Prison Service and were reflected in practice, the rule suggested by the May Committee would fall into place as an attempt to define what those values imply. A rule embodying the idea of 'humane containment' would also fit naturally into a context of moral purpose that distinguishes human beings from animals. The public ought also to take its proper share of responsibility for how society permits people to be treated in prison and after release.

This is not Nazi Germany, nor is our society unfree, nor are the vast majority of our people unkindly. (So far as prison is concerned, they are merely unthinking, and that is partly the fault of politicians and civil servants – perhaps even the media – for not putting prisons higher on the nation's agenda.) Yet our government is on the whole usually more tolerant than many extremists would have us believe, even if, like a reluctant donkey, it needs goading from time to time.

But the extreme lesson of Nazi Germany should never be forgotten. Down the road of public apathy in the 1930s lay Auschwitz and Buchenwald.

Prisons are above all a moral issue and must remain so.

Appendix
List of Members of the May Committee

Mr Justice May
Mr Justice May became a judge of the High Court, Queen's Bench Division, in 1972 and was presiding judge of the Midland and Oxford Circuit between 1973 and 1977. Educated as Balliol College, he is aged fifty-six, was knighted in 1972, and is a member of the Parole Board.

Mrs Dorothy Bellerby
Mrs Bellerby is fifty-seven years old. She is a JP, a past leader of the Labour group of the Surrey County Council, a Guildford District Councillor, and Mayoress of Guildford. She is active in social work at the national as well as the local level.

Mr Michael Bett
Mr Bett is in his mid-forties and is Director of Personnel at the BBC.

Mr Leonard Edmondson
Mr Edmondson is sixty-five. He is a former Executive Council Member of the AUEW and a Member of the General Council of the TUC.

Mrs Rachel Gibbs, JP
Rachel Gibbs is forty-eight. She is a former Chairman of the Board of Visitors and member of the Local Review Committee at Swinfen Hall Prison and is at present a member of the Board of Visitors at Pentonville Prison.

Mr Nicholas Hinton
Mr Hinton is thirty-six. He is Director of the National Council of Social Service and a former Director of the National Association for the Care and Resettlement of Offenders.

Sir Myles Humphreys

Sir Myles Humphreys is fifty-three. He is a former Lord Mayor of Belfast, Chairman of the Northern Ireland Police Authority, and a former Chairman of the Board of Visitors to Belfast Prison.

Sheriff C. G. B. Nicholson

Mr Nicholson is forty-three. He is Sheriff of the Lothians in Edinburgh Sheriff Court. He is active in penal matters as a member of the Scottish Council on Crime, a member of the Dunpark Committee on Reparation by the Offender, and Chairman of the Scottish Association for the Study of Delinquency.

Sir John Nightingale

Sir John Nightingale is sixty-five. He is a member of the Parole Board and a former Chief Constable of Essex and Chairman of the Police Council.

Mr J. A. Gardiner

Mr Gardiner is forty. He is Managing Director of the Laird Group, a member of the National Enterprise Board Organisation Committee and of British Airways Board, and a Director of British Leyland.

References

GENERAL

References to evidence given to 'MPs' or to 'the Expenditure Committee'
These refer to the Expenditure Committee of the House of Commons, volumes II and III, Minutes of Evidence, Fifteenth Report of the Expenditure Committee, Session 1977–8, *The Reduction of Pressure on the Prison System* (HMSO).

However, similar references in Chapter 6, 'Women in Prison', are to evidence to the same committee which was not published in an omnibus edition because of the intervention of the 1979 general election. The evidence is to be found in reports under the general heading: Expenditure Committee, Minutes of Evidence, Session 1978–9, *Women and the Penal System*. The reports are dated as follows:

20 November 1978	Home Office
4 December 1978	Howard League for Penal Reform; NACRO
11 December 1978	Boards of Visitors
22 January 1979	National Association of Probation Officers; Prison and Borstal Governors' branch of the Society of Civil and Public Servants
25 January 1979	HM Prison Holloway; The Baroness Vickers, Miss H. Buckingham, Miss S. James, and Miss Kim L.
29 January 1979	Conference of Chief Probation Officers; Prison Officers' Association
4 February 1979	HM Prison Styal
5 February 1979	Professor T. C. N. Gibbens
12 February 1979	Mr Leo Abse MP
21 February 1979	Mr Charles Irving MP
22 Februarhy 1979	HM Borstal Bullwood Hall
12 March 1979	Association of Chief Police Officers of England, Wales and Northern Ireland; Police Federation
26 March 1979	Metropolitan Police

Full details of works referred to in the text, given in the order in which they are first referred to.

References 163

page	line	
		CHAPTER 1
5	14	Richard Friedenthal, *Luther, sein Leben und sein Zeit* (1967, R. Piper & Co. Verlag); English translation by John Nowell (1970, Weidenfeld & Nicolson)
5	17	See Pauline Gregg, *The Welfare State* (1967, Harrap) and R. C. Birch, *The Shaping of the Welfare State* (1974, Longman)
5	21	G. W. Pailthorpe MD, *What we put in prison and preventive and rescue homes* (1932, Williams & Norgate Ltd)
6	30	See Marcel Berlins and Geoffrey Wansell, *Caught in the Act: Children, Society and the Law* (1974, Pelican)
10	28	See Philip John Stead, ed., *Pioneers in Policing* (1977, Patterson Smith, NJ, USA; McGraw-Hill UK Ltd)
		CHAPTER 2
14	27	The figures are from *Prison Statistics of England and Wales 1978* (1979, HMSO)
14	30	Roy D. King and Rodney Morgan, *A Taste of Prison* (Routledge Direct Editions)
		CHAPTER 3
23	29	Home Office Research Study No. 51, *Life Sentence Prisoners* (1979, HMSO)
24	14	Home Office, *Prisons and the Prisoner* (1977, HMSO)
26	32	Advisory Council on the Penal System, *Sentences of Imprisonment* (HMSO)
28	3	Lord Mountbatten of Burma, Report of the Inquiry into Prison Escapes and Security, Cmnd 3175 (1966, HMSO)
28	36	Advisory Council on the Penal System, *The Regime for Long-Term Prisoners in Conditions of Maximum Security* (HMSO)
29	27	Mr Abse is quoted in J. E. Hall Williams, *Changing Prisons* (1975, Peter Owen)
30	7	White Paper, *Penal Practice in a Changing Society*, Cmnd 645 (1959, HMSO)
31	30	*Prison Statistics England and Wales 1977*, Cmnd 7286 (1978, HMSO)
		CHAPTER 4
33	6	Home Office, *Report on the Work of the Prison Department 1976*, Cmnd 6877 (HMSO)

page	line	
34	12	Larry O. Gostin, *A Human Condition: The law relating to mentally abnormal offenders*, vol. 2, *Observations, analysis and proposals for reform* (1977, MIND)
36	23	D. J. West, *The Habitual Prisoner* (1963, Macmillan)
39	18	Lord Butler of Saffron Walden, Interim Report of the Committee on Mentally Abnormal Offenders, Cmnd 5698 (1974, HMSO)

CHAPTER 5

45	19	A. E. Bottoms and F. H. McClintock, *Criminals Coming of Age* (1975, Heinemann Educational Books)
45	25	Pat Cawson, Young Offenders in Care, preliminary report, (1978, DHSS)
46	32	Dartington Social Research Centre, *Locking Up Children* (1978, Saxton House)
47	10	Quoted in Leon Radzinowicz and Joan King, *The growth of crime: The international experience* (1977, Hamish Hamilton; 1979, Pelican)
48	10	D. J. West and D. P. Farrington, *Who becomes delinquent?* (1973, Heinemann Educational Books)
49	18	Dr Melitta Schmideberg, 'Juvenile Murderers' *International Journal of Offender Therapy and Comparative Criminology* (Association for the Psychiatric Treatment of Offenders), Volume 17, No. 3, 1973

CHAPTER 6

59	1	Home Office, *Treatment of Women and Girls in Custody* (1970, HMSO)
59	26	C. I. Nawby, 'Sexual Discrimination and the Law', *Probation Journal*, June 1977
61	25	C Gibbs, 'The Effect of Imprisonment of Women Upon their Children', *British Journal of Criminology*, April 1971
61	31	Home Office, *Treatment of Women and Girls in Custody* (1970, HMSO)
63	20	T. C. N. Gibbens, 'Female Offenders', *British Journal of Hospital Medicine*, September 1971
65	3	*The Yorkshire Post*, 5 January 1976

CHAPTER 7

66	17	See J. E. Hall Williams, *Changing Prisons* (1975, Peter Owen)

References 165

page	line	
66	22	See Jorgen Jepsen, 'KRIM, KRUM and KROM', *Prison Service Journal*, October 1971
76	28	Reported in the Daily Telegraph, 16 December 1978
81	8	Reported in *The Guardian*, 30 January 1979

CHAPTER 8

85	14	Roy King and Kenneth W. Elliott, *Albany: Birth of a Prison – End of an Era* (Routledge & Kegan Paul)
86	37	G. Fowler, Report of an Inquiry by the Chief Inspector of the Prison Service into the cause and the circumstances of the events at HM Prison Hull during the period 31 August to 3 September 1976
91	36	Reported in the *Daily Telegraph*, 17 January 1979
92	1	Reported in *The Guardian*, 17 January 1979

CHAPTER 9

94	24	Reported by David Beresford in *The Guardian*, 19 April 1979
99	25	Mr Daniel was reported in *The Times*, 15 July 1977
102	30	Reported in *The Times*, 24 April 1978

CHAPTER 10

110	7	May Inquiry, Evidence from the Prison and Borstal Governors (England and Wales) branch of the Society of Civil and Public Servants

CHAPTER 11

146	25	Payne Committee, *Report of the Committee on the Enforcement of Judgement Debts*, Cmnd 3909 (1969, HMSO)
148	5	Howard League, *Howard Journal*, Vol. 19, No. 1, 1980